LITURGIAM AUTHENTICAM

FIFTH INSTRUCTION ON VERNACULAR TRANSLATION OF THE ROMAN LITURGY

LITURGIAM AUTHENTICAM

FIFTH INSTRUCTION ON VERNACULAR TRANSLATION OF THE ROMAN LITURGY

Congregation for Divine Worship and
the Discipline of the Sacraments

United States Conference of Catholic Bishops • Washington, D.C.

This resource volume entitled *Liturgiam authenticam* presents a translation of the *Fifth Instruction for the Right Application of the Constitution on the Sacred Liturgy of the Second Vatican Council (Sacrosanctum Concilium, art. 36)*. This fifth Instruction was issued by the Congregation for Divine Worship and the Discipline of the Sacraments on March 28, 2001. The USCCB Committee on the Liturgy has provided this facing-page translation—together with the appendix materials, *Varietates legitimae* and the Vatican press release of May 7, 2001, on the Instruction—under the direction of its chairman, Archbishop Oscar H. Lipscomb, who authored the Introduction and approved the final editing of the texts. This publication is authorized by the undersigned.

Monsignor William P. Fay
General Secretary
USCCB

Cover: *St. Jerome* by Caravaggio (1573-1610). Galleria Borghese, Rome, Italy. Copyright © Scala/Art Resource, N.Y.

The English translation of the Address of Pope Paul VI to Translators of Liturgical Texts (10 November 1965) from *Documents on the Liturgy 1963-1979: Conciliar, Papal, and Curial Texts* © 1982, International Committee on English in the Liturgy, Inc. All rights reserved.

First Printing, November 2001

ISBN 1-57455-428-X

The time has come to renew that spirit which inspired the Church at the moment when the Constitution Sacrosanctum Concilium was prepared, discussed, voted upon and promulgated and when the first steps were taken to apply it. The seed was sown: it has known the rigors of winter, but the seed has sprouted, and become a tree. It is a matter of the organic growth of a tree becoming ever stronger the deeper it sinks its roots into the soil of tradition. . . . In the work of liturgical renewal, desired by the Council, it is necessary to keep in mind "with great balance the part of God and the part of man, the hierarchy and the faithful, tradition and progress, the law and adaptation, the individual and the community, silence and choral praise. Thus the Liturgy on earth will fuse with that of heaven, where . . . it will form one choir . . . to praise with one voice the Father through Jesus Christ."

—John Paul II, *Vicesimus quintus annus*:
On the Twenty-Fifth Anniversary of the Constitution on the Sacred Liturgy
December 4, 1988

CONTENTS

INTRODUCTION

~

ARCHBISHOP OSCAR H. LIPSCOMB
CHAIRMAN, BISHOPS' COMMITTEE ON THE LITURGY

Rome was quiet in the second week of May 1989. A younger, vigorous John Paul II had just returned from Madagascar, Malawi, Reunion, and Zambia—his forty-first papal visit. Little noticed, then, was the release of an important apostolic letter, *Vicesimus quintus annus*, which would mark the twenty-fifth anniversary of the conciliar promulgation of *Sacrosanctum Concilium*, the watershed document of Vatican II, which directed the reform of the liturgy of the Roman rite. At the same time, *Vicesimus quintus annus* called for the Church to address her need for renewal again, this time by re-examining the path of the liturgical reform already taken, compounding efforts where clearly successful, and targeting areas fraught with difficulties.

John Paul II singled out several problems for frank discussion: the invention or manipulation of rites outside the framework of the established reform; the inadequate reception of the liturgical books—either by those who reject all but the pre-conciliar rites as a sole guarantee of true faith, or by others who are indifferent to the official reform, substituting their own innovations instead—and a continued confusion between the ministerial and baptismal priesthoods. It is for the bishop, he concluded, to address liturgical practice in his own diocese, since "the life of the faithful in Christ in some sense is derived from and depends upon him" (no. 13). A decade later, it is clear that the direction John Paul II offered in *Vicesimus quintus annus* has become a part of the framework for the continued reform of the liturgy. We turn now to examine two essential points taken from his letter that constitute part of the fundamental message of *Liturgiam authenticam*.

Two Essential Points

The many important ideas of *Liturgiam authenticam* can be found in excellent summary form in recent issues of the *Bishops Committee on the Liturgy Newsletter* (37 [April-May 2001]: 14-18). As well, the Vatican website has provided a background piece—included in Appendix A in this volume—relative to the development of the publication of the Instruction, with its own summary of *Liturgiam authenticam*. Two points in particular appear to be of great significance and deserve some detailed discussion here.

It is perhaps the first and most important message of *Liturgiam authenticam* that bishops and episcopal conferences must take responsibility for the reform of the liturgy and, in particular, for the preparation and publication of liturgical books. *Liturgiam authenticam* states plainly that, in the first order, the reform of the liturgy is entrusted to the bishops (no. 3). It is now, for example, the duty of the episcopal conference to establish its liturgical commission with bishop members (no. 70). Bishops of each region, usually through their episcopal conference, must devise a pastoral plan for the use of the vernacular in their churches (no. 10). Only the diocesan bishop may grant permission for other languages to be used in his diocese in the celebration of the liturgy (no. 18). All the bishops of a given territory are now to discuss the revisions of liturgical language proposed for liturgical books (no. 21). Conferences of bishops are to see to the publication of "an integral translation of the Sacred Scriptures intended for the private study and reading of the faithful" (no. 36). Bishops are to guard against translations that are not truly a common effort and are, instead, the work of "any one person or of a small group of persons" (no. 72). Such conferences demonstrate their fraternal bond with the See of Peter when they submit all prepared liturgical books for the required *recognitio* (no. 80). Bishops of different regions in which the same language is spoken are to arrange a common translation of liturgical books (no. 87); should this prove impossible, conferences of bishops may choose to adapt appropriately for their own regions (no. 87). Bishops should always participate in the various stages of preparation of a text up to its submission to the full conference of bishops (no. 97). Individual conferences of bishops may establish commissions for the creation of new texts in the vernacular (no. 106).

Surely, however, the most demanding statement of episcopal responsibility is found in no. 70 and is addressed to every bishop personally: "With respect to the examination and approbation of the [liturgical] texts, each and every Bishop must commit himself to this as a direct, solemn and personal responsibility." Here it is the clear intention of the Instruction to state that every bishop member of a given episcopal conference must shoulder the responsibility for the approval of liturgical texts. No liturgical committee, translation body, scholarly organization, conference structure, or mixed commission may take the place of the judgment of the bishop members of a conference when, as individuals, they vote on the suitability of proposed liturgical texts. According to given circumstances, then, every bishop must assume the burden of his own education in these matters at least commensurate with his voting responsibilities.

The second point of urgency in *Liturgiam authenticam* regards the proper way in which liturgical vernacularization is to be understood as belonging to a category of theological enterprise introduced by the Council itself. For this discussion, a greater introduction is needed.

In retrospect, we can see clearly that the desire for the use of the vernacular in the liturgy is a conversation that has been ongoing since the Council itself. Indeed, the question of whether to use vernacular languages in the liturgy dates, in the modern period, from the Council of Trent (1545-1552), which forbade its use in the face of Protestant reforms meant to deny Catholic teaching (Council of Trent, Session 22, [September 17, 1562], especially chapters 8-9, *Canones de Sanctissimo missae Sacrificio*, no. 9). However, by the start of the liturgical movement in the twentieth century, made popular through the great figures of Prosper Gueranger, Lambert Beaduin, Josef Jungmann, Godfrey Diekmann, Louis Bouyer, and others, new momentum built to suggest that pastorally and liturgically the Church was now ready at least to experiment with the vernacular.

The intense examination of the problem at the Council resulted in the sections of *Sacrosanctum Concilium* (nos. 36, 38, 54) that opened the Church to the celebration of the entire sacramental economy in vernacular languages. It is Paul VI's memorable statement which reminds us that in the full use of the vernacular, "the translations now have become part of the rites themselves; they have become the voice of the Church" (Address to Translators of Liturgical Texts, November 10, 1965; in *Documents on the Liturgy 1963- 1979: Conciliar, Papal, and Curial Texts* [DOL] [Collegeville, Minn.: Liturgical Press, 1982]). Vernacularization is a permanent part of the Roman rite.

Contrary to a common impression, however, there have been many documents from the Holy See between the time of the Second Vatican Council and the present, tracing the continuous path of experimentation that vernacularization has followed in the Roman Church. John Paul II's *Vicesimus quintus annus* marks little more than the halfway point in this journey. Indeed, between the December 1963 vote on *Sacrosanctum Concilium* and the 1978 election of John Paul II, no fewer than forty separate documents regulating the translation and publication of liturgical books were issued by the pope or a dicastery of the Holy See.

By far, the most significant of these was *Comme le prévoit*, released in its official French text by the Consilium in January 1969, some six years after the Conciliar decision to permit vernacularization. Formally entitled as an Instruction "On the Translation of Liturgical Texts for the Celebration [of Mass] with a Congregation," *Comme le prévoit* captured what many felt at the time was the exact spirit in which modern translation of the liturgy should be done: "Thus in the case of liturgical communication, it is necessary to take into account not only the message to be conveyed, but also the speaker, the audience, and the style. Translations, therefore, must be faithful to the art of communication in all its various aspects, but especially in regard to the message itself, in regard to the audience for which it is intended, and in regard to the manner of expression" (no. 7). It has been in view of this principle—with its multiple elements respecting the complexities of literary composition, orality, semantics, linguistic anthroplogy, and what theorists refer to as the "performance dimensions" of translations, i.e., the ability of a translated prayer to convey to its *hearers* (rather than its *readers*) through apt proclamation the meaning of an original text—that the International Commission on English in the

Liturgy (ICEL) has produced substantial translations of the
Roman Missal and most of the sacraments.

In the thirty-two years since the publication of *Comme le
prévoit*, however, many aspects of its implicit translation
theory have been tested against two key challenges that have
shaped the conversation on vernacularization: (1) inculturation, or the "incarnation of the Gospel in autonomous
cultures and at the same time, the introduction of these
cultures into the life of the Church" (*Varietates legitimae*,
no. 4), especially as regards the use of languages other than
Latin in the liturgy; and (2) fidelity not only between the
original Latin text and the vernacular as expressions of the
same content of faith, but also fidelity with the spirit and
style of the Roman rite. It is one of the express purposes of
Liturgiam authenticam to address these two issues in detail
(nos. 1-9) and thereby "to prepare a new era of liturgical
renewal, which is consonant with the qualities and the traditions of the particular Churches, but which safeguards also
the faith and the unity of the whole Church of God" (no. 7).

It is therefore important to note how *Liturgiam authenticam*
ties its own message closely to that of *Varietates legitimae*:
"The norms set forth in this Instruction are to be substituted
for all norms previously published on the matter, with the
exception of the Instruction *Varietates legitimae*, published by
the Congregation for Divine Worship and the Discipline of
the Sacraments on January 25, 1994, in conjunction with

which the norms in this present Instruction are to be understood. The norms contained in this Instruction are to be considered applicable to the translation of texts intended for liturgical use in the Roman Rite and, *mutatis mutandis*, in the other duly recognized Rites of the Latin Church" (no. 8). In short, it is perhaps the second most important message of *Liturgiam authenticam* that vernacularization is to be understood theologically and primarily through the lens of inculturation, as a working category of the Conciliar theological reform.

History of the Discussion on English Translation Since Vatican Council II

Certainly since the approval of the English translation of the *Order of Christian Funerals* in 1989, and then again with the resolution to the many issues that surfaced in connection with gaining the *recognitio* for the revised *Lectionary for Mass*, the United States Conference of Catholic Bishops (USCCB) has engaged the Congregation for Divine Worship and the Discipline of the Sacraments as well as ICEL in a vigorous dialogue regarding principles of liturgical translation. It is enough to recall, in connection with the problem of inclusive language in biblical readings intended for liturgical use, the 1990 guidelines devised by this Conference, entitled *Criteria for the Evaluation of Inclusive Language Translations of Scriptural Texts Proposed for Liturgical Use*. In addition, the episcopal conference of the United States held three separate fora on translation, beginning with a special study day in La Jolla, California, in 1994, followed by a second session on translation with ICEL officials in June 1996, and concluding with the November 1998 Forum on Translation, organized in Washington, D.C., for the benefit of all bishops who wished to attend.

As the *Lectionary* task group of Archbishops Jerome G. Hanus, OSB, Justin Rigali, and William J. Levada was concluding its work with the Congregation for the Doctrine of the Faith (CDF) and the Congregation for Divine Worship and the Discipline of the Sacraments (CDWDS), a June 13, 1996, letter from then-Archbishop Geraldo Majello Agnelo, archbishop-secretary of CDWDS, was addressed to the episcopal board of ICEL. The letter stated that while *Comme le prévoit* did indeed contain important principles of liturgical trans-lation, it was nonetheless the opinion of the Congregation that this 1969 Instruction was in need of review. On February 1, 1997, Cardinal Angelo Sodano, Secretary of State, released a letter from the Supreme Pontiff to Cardinal Arturo Medina Estevez, Prefect of CDWDS, mandating the development of a new document on the translation of liturgical texts.

While these constituted many of the public discussions regarding the principles of translation that led to the publication of *Liturgiam authenticam*, an even more intense debate was taking place between the Bishops' Committee on the Liturgy

(BCL), the CDWDS and a broad spectrum of scholars involved in the "Consultation on Translation" sponsored by the BCL. A series of meetings between the BCL Secretariat and officials of the CDWDS, together with written consultation reports from more than twenty American, British, Australian, and Canadian liturgists, resulted in a two-part report entitled "A Consultation on Translation" submitted to the BCL in the fall of 1998. Many of the same issues that are now discussed in *Liturgiam authenticam* were, as careful review demonstrates, raised repeatedly in each of these special discussions which intensified from the early 1990s. A partial timeline of translation discussions and documents from 1963 to 2001 is appended to this introduction.

Pastoral Implementation

As definitive a statement as *Liturgiam authenticam* may be, however, its pastoral implementation yet awaits us. Central to this is the development of two important documents that, for each bishops' conference, will help in large measure to determine that implementation. The first is the *ratio translationis*, or schema for the application of each vernacular language to the Roman liturgy. *Liturgiam authenticam*, no. 9, describes this *ratio* as a description of how the principles of translation within the Instruction are to be applied to a particular vernacular. As well, *Liturgiam authenticam*, no. 10, requires that each region or episcopal conference devise a pastoral plan for the use of vernacular languages in its territories.

In addition, the complex questions raised regarding the use of the Neo-Vulgate as a guide in the translation of biblical texts intended for liturgical use will demand textual expertise and pastoral care for an effective implementation. Unexpected problems—such as how to make use of the best translations of the Wisdom literature, taken from Hebrew, Syriac, or Greek texts, which differ so markedly from that of the Neo-Vulgate—will call for the concerted effort of scholars in many fields. Further questions in the contextualization of ecumenical and interfaith concerns—such as are raised in *Liturgiam authenticam*, no. 29, for example, regarding the choice of one translation over another in expressions relative to the Jews—will benefit from research that harmonizes the guidelines of the Instruction with the Conciliar teachings of *Nostra aetate* and the papacy of John Paul II.

Facing-Page Translation of the USCCB

The re-edited text of the Instruction found in the present edition is provided for readers who appreciate the use of a facing-page translation. For whenever a source language is positioned next to its target or translation language, the two can be seen immediately to be in a kind of dialogue. The process of inculturation that now defines liturgical translation is more clearly seen in this way.

After review by the USCCB Secretariat for the Liturgy, the unofficial English translation of *Liturgiam authenticam*, as provided by the Vatican Press Office on the Vatican's website, was edited with the assistance of officials of the Congregation for Divine Worship and the Discipline of the Sacraments. The present text is the result of this process.

In addition to the text of the Instruction, it was felt that two appendix texts would be of assistance to the reader. First, the background material offered by the Holy See in its press release as an introduction to its presentation of the Latin text of *Liturgiam authenticam* on the Vatican website is included. Second, the all-important text of *Varietates legitimae*—the fourth Instruction on inculturation, which is now to be read in tandem with *Liturgiam authenticam*—is provided. Both of these pieces make for profitable reading in concert with the text of the fifth Instruction.

Conclusion

As the most recent statement on translation from the Holy See, *Liturgiam authenticam* represents important developments in implementing the immense task of vernacularization that the Second Vatican Council undertook so enthusiastically nearly forty years ago. It is hoped that this re-edited translation, together with its appendix materials, may offer the reader some support and insight into understanding the joys and difficulties that the reformed liturgy, particularly in its inculturated use of the vernacular, presents to the Church today. Let us keep before us the words of

Pope Paul VI, who, with the Council fathers, opened the Church to expressing its full voice in prayer through every human tongue:

> Like a caring mother, the Church, through the teaching of Vatican Council II, has called on its children, in full awareness of their responsibility in the Body of Christ, to share actively in the liturgical prayers and rites. For this reason, the Church has permitted the translation of texts venerable for their antiquity, devotion, beauty, and long-standing use. That is proof of the exalted duty and weighty responsibilities of those who translate such texts. The translations published here and there prior to the promulgation of the Constitution on the Liturgy had as their purpose to assist the faithful's understanding of the rite celebrated in Latin; they were aids to people untrained in this ancient language. The translations now, however, have become part of the rites themselves; they have become the voice of the Church. (Paul VI, Address to Translators of Liturgical Texts, November 10, 1965; in DOL)

† Most Rev. Oscar H. Lipscomb
Mobile, Alabama
Chairman, Bishops' Committee on the Liturgy

Chronological Select List of Documents on Liturgical Translation from the Holy See and the USCCB, 1963-2001

VATICAN COUNCIL II, Constitution on the Liturgy *Sacrosanctum Concilium* (December 4, 1963).

CONSILIUM and SACRED CONGREGATION (SC) FOR RITES, Instruction (first), *Inter oecumenici*, general principles for carrying out of the liturgical renewal (September 26, 1964).

CONSILIUM, Letter, *Consilium ad exsequendum*, to the conferences of bishops, on uniform translations in a common language (October 16, 1964).

PAUL VI, Remarks at the Angelus, on beginning of the vernacular in the liturgy (March 7, 1965).

SECRETARIAT OF STATE, Letter, *Ho L'onore*, in Pope Paul VI's concession of the preface in the vernacular (April 27, 1965).

CONSILIUM, Instruction, *Popularibus interpretationibus*, on translations of propers of dioceses and religious families (June 1-2, 1965).

SC RITES, Enumeration, *Constitutio de sacra Liturgia*, of the parts of rites of ordination in the vernacular (July 17, 1965).

PAUL VI, Address to translators of liturgical texts (November 10, 1965).

SC RITES and SC RELIGIOUS, Instruction, *In edicendis normis*, on language to be used in celebrations of religious (November 23, 1965).

CONSILIUM, Reply (U.S.A.), on Mass for the deaf (December 10, 1965).

CONSILIUM, Communication, *Per Litteras Apostolicas*, on norms for translation of the Mass of the Jubilee (January 21, 1966).

SC RITES, (Consilium), Decree, *Cum nostra aetate*, on editions of liturgical books (January 27, 1966).

PAUL VI, Address to Latinists (April 16, 1966).

SC RITES, Letter, *Non latet sane* to the conferences of bishops, on royalties for Latin liturgical books (August 5, 1966).

ADMINISTRATION OF THE PATRIMONY OF THE HOLY SEE, Letter to the conferences of bishops on royalties for liturgical books (September 10, 1966).

PAUL VI, Concession, allowing *ad experimentum*, vernacular in the Canon of the Mass and in ordinations (January 31, 1967).

SC RITES (Consilium), Instruction (second), *Tres abhinc annos*, on carrying out the Constitution on the Liturgy (May 4, 1967).

CONSILIUM, Communication, *Aussitot apres*, to the conferences of bishops on the translation of the Roman Canon (August 10, 1967).

SC RELIGIOUS, Rescript, (Capuchins), on the vernacular in the divine office (September 20, 1967).

ADMINISTRATION OF THE PATRIMONY OF THE HOLY SEE, Letter to the conferences of bishops on royalties for liturgical books (January 8, 1968).

CONSILIUM, Communication, *Instantibus pluribus*, on norms for the translation of the *Gradule simplex* (January 23, 1968).

PAUL VI, Address to Latinists, on Latin and the vernacular in the Church (April 26, 1968).

CONSILIUM, Instruction, *Comme le prévoit,* on translation of liturgical texts for celebrations with a congregation (January 25, 1969).

CONSILIUM, Declaration, *Circa instructionem,* on *ad interim* translations of liturgical texts (March 1969).

SC DIVINE WORSHIP, Declaration, *Plures liturgicae,* on the translation of new liturgical texts (September 15, 1969).

SC DIVINE WORSHIP, Letter, *Cum nonnullae Conferentiae,* to the conferences of bishops on Latin appendix to vernacular Roman Missals (November 10, 1969).

SC DIVINE WORSHIP, Norms *in confirmandis actis,* on uniform translations of liturgical texts (February 6, 1970).

SC DIVINE WORSHIP, Letter, *Tandis que cette S. Congregation,* to the conferences of bishops, on the publication of liturgical books (February 25, 1970).

SC DIVINE WORSHIP, Declaration, *Nonnullae commissiones,* on the publication of liturgical books (May 15, 1970).

SC DIVINE WORSHIP, Letter, *Die 2 Februarii,* to liturgical commissions, on the vernacular translation of the rite of religious profession (July 15, 1970).

SC DIVINE WORSHIP, Instruction (third), *Liturgicae instaurationes,* on the carrying out of the Constitution on the Liturgy (September 5, 1970).

SC DIVINE WORSHIP, Letter, *Al comenzar,* to conferences of bishops of Spanish-speaking countries, on translations (October 29, 1971).

SC DIVINE WORSHIP, Circular Letter, *El 6 febrero*, to Spanish-speaking conferences of bishops in Latin America, on uniform translations (November 20, 1972).

SC DIVINE WORSHIP, Note, *Liturgiae horarum interpretationes*, on vernacular editions of *The Liturgy of the Hours* (January 15, 1973).

SC DIVINE WORSHIP, Circular Letter, *Dum toto terrarum*, to the conferences of bishops, on the translation of the forms of the sacraments (October 25, 1973).

SC DOCTRINE OF THE FAITH, Declaration, *Instauratio liturgica*, on the translation of the forms of the sacraments (January 25, 1974).

SC DOCTRINE OF THE FAITH, Letter to Cardinal F. Marty, on the preparation of the vernacular editions of the rite of penance (June 3, 1974).

SC DIVINE WORSHIP, Letter to presidents of English-speaking conferences, approving the translation of the sacramental form for Confirmation (May 5, 1975).

SC DIVINE WORSHIP, Note, *Passim quaeritur*, on music in vernacular editions of the Roman Missal (May 1975).

SC DIVINE WORSHIP, SC SACRAMENTS AND DIVINE WORSHIP, Letter, *Decem iam annos*, to the conferences of bishops, on the vernacular in the liturgy (June 5, 1976).

JOHN PAUL II, Apostolic Letter, *Patres ecclesiae*, on the sixteenth centenary of the death of St. Basil, with excerpts regarding liturgy and language (January 2, 1980).

CODE OF CANON LAW, Canons regarding liturgical books, their preparation and translation (January 25, 1983).

SC SACRAMENTS AND DIVINE WORSHIP, Communication on decisions of the SC Doctrine of the Faith concerning the translation of *carnis resurrectionem* in the Apostles' Creed (December 1983).

JOHN PAUL II, Encyclical, *Slavorum apostoli*, regarding the use of the vernacular in the liturgy and on inculturation as realized by Cyril and Methodius (June 2, 1985).

JOHN PAUL II, Apostolic Letter, *Euntes in mundum*, on the occasion of the millennial anniversary of the Baptism of the Keivan Rus' with excerpts on liturgical language and inculturation (January 25, 1988).

JOHN PAUL II, Apostolic Constitution, *Pastor Bonus*, on the reorganization of the Roman Curia, art. 62, regarding the Congregation for Divine Worship and the Discipline of the Sacraments (June 28, 1988).

JOHN PAUL II, Apostolic letter, *Vicesimus quintus annus*, on the twenty-fifth anniversary of the Constitution on the Sacred Liturgy, *Sacrosanctum Concilium* (December 4, 1988).

NATIONAL CONFERENCE OF CATHOLIC BISHOPS (NCCB), *Criteria for the Evaluation of Inclusive Language Translations of Scripture Texts Proposed for Liturgical Use* (November 15, 1990).

PONTIFICAL COUNCIL FOR THE PROMOTION OF CHRISTIAN UNITY, Directory, *La recherche de l'unité*, for the application of the principles and norms on ecumenism, with excerpts on the communion of life and spiritual activity among the baptized (March 25, 1993).

JOHN PAUL II, Address to a group of Bishops from the United States, on the occasion of their *ad limina* visit, excerpt on the translation of liturgical texts (December 4, 1993).

CONGREGATION (CG) FOR DIVINE WORSHIP AND DISCIPLINE OF THE SACRAMENTS, Instruction (fourth), *Varietates legitimae,* for the correct application of the conciliar Constitution on the Sacred Liturgy, on the Roman liturgy and inculturation (January 25, 1994).

NCCB, Study day on liturgical translation in La Jolla, Calif.: *Principles of Translation: Issues in the Application of the Hermeneutics of "Comme le prévoit,"* by D. McManus in *Bishops' Committee on the Liturgy Newletter* (30 [June-July 1994]: 166-170) (June 23, 1994).

CG DIVINE WORSHIP AND DISCIPLINE OF THE SACRAMENTS, Letter to ICEL Episcopal Board regarding the need for new norms for liturgical translation (June 13, 1996).

NCCB, Study day on liturgical translation in Portland, Ore. (June 20, 1996).

JOHN PAUL II, Letter to Cardinal A. Medina Estevez, Prefect of Congregation for Divine Worship and Discipline of the Sacraments, mandating the composition of norms for liturgical translation (February 1, 1997).

NCCB, BISHOPS' COMMITTEE ON THE LITURGY, *Consultation on the Translation of Liturgical Texts* (June 1, 1998).

NCCB, AD HOC COMMITTEE ON THE FORUM ON THE PRINCIPLES OF TRANSLATION, *The Voice of the Church* (Washington, D.C.: United States Catholic Conference, 2001) (November 20, 1998).

CG DIVINE WORSHIP AND DISCIPLINE OF THE SACRAMENTS, Instruction (fifth), *Liturgiam authenticam,* On the use of vernacular languages in the publication of the books of the Roman Liturgy (March 28, 2001).

LITURGIAM
AUTHENTICAM

DE USU LINGUARUM POPULARIUM IN LIBRIS LITURGIAE ROMANAE EDENDIS

INSTRUCTIO QUINTA

«AD EXSECUTIONEM CONSTITUTIONIS
CONCILII VATICANI SECUNDI
DE SACRA LITURGIA RECTA ORDINANDAM»

(AD CONST. ART. 36)

1. Liturgiam authenticam, e viva et vetustissima spirituali traditione Ecclesiae exortam, valde optavit Sacrosanctum Concilium Oecumenicum Vaticanum Secundum studiose custodire atque ingenio variorum populorum pastorali cum sapientia accommodare, ita ut fideles in plena, conscia et actuosa participatione sacrarum actionum, praecipue in Sacramentorum celebratione, uberem fontem gratiarum et facultatem se continenter formandi ad mysterium christianum invenirent.[1]

---

1   Cf. CONC. OECUM. VAT. II, Const. de S. Liturgia *Sacrosanctum Concilium*, nn. 1, 14, 21, 33; cf. CONC. OECUM. TRID., Sess. XXII, diei 17 septembris 1562, Doctr. *De ss. Missae sacrif.*, c. 8: Denz.-Schönm. n. 1749.

ON THE USE OF VERNACULAR LANGUAGES IN THE PUBLICATION OF THE BOOKS OF THE ROMAN LITURGY

LITURGIAM AUTHENTICAM: FIFTH INSTRUCTION
"FOR THE RIGHT IMPLEMENTATION OF THE
CONSTITUTION ON THE SACRED LITURGY OF
THE SECOND VATICAN COUNCIL"
(SACROSANCTUM CONCILIUM, ART. 36)

1. The Second Vatican Council strongly desired to preserve with care the authentic Liturgy, which flows forth from the Church's living and most ancient spiritual tradition, and to adapt it with pastoral wisdom to the genius of the various peoples so that the faithful might find in their full, conscious, and active participation in the sacred actions—especially the celebration of the Sacraments—an abundant source of graces and a means for their own continual formation in the Christian mystery.[1]

---

1   Second Vatican Council, Const. on the Sacred Liturgy *Sacrosanctum Concilium*, nn. 1, 14, 21, 33; cf. Council of Trent, Sess. XXII, 17 September 1562, Doctr. *De ss. Missae sacrif.*, c. 8: Denz.-Schönm. n. 1749.

2. Exinde, Summorum Pontificum cura, magnum opus instaurandi libros liturgicos Ritus romani coepit initium, quod amplectebatur translationem[2] in sermones populares eo consilio ut instauratio diligentissima sacrae Liturgiae efficeretur, scilicet unum ex praecipuis praedicti Concilii propositis.

3. Instauratio liturgica usque adhuc prosperos eventus habuit opera et ingenio multorum, praesertim Episcoporum, quorum curae ac studio magnum hoc ac difficile munus est commissum. Pariter maxima prudentia et cura postulantur in libris liturgicis apparandis, qui sint sana doctrina insignes, in elocutione accurati, immunes omni effectu ideologico atque ceterum iis praediti qualitatibus, quibus sacra mysteria salutis et indefectibilis fides Ecclesiae in orationem efficaciter transmittatur humana lingua, et cultus idoneus Deo Altissimo exhibeatur.[3]

---

2   Textus quidem in aliam linguam redditus saepius vocabulis «versio», «conversio», «interpretatio», «redditio», vel etiam «mutatio» aut «transductio» latine designatur, ipsa vero actio seu gestus sic faciendi verbis affinibus exprimitur. Quod in Constitutione «*Sacrosanctum Concilium*» perplurimisque documentis Sanctae Sedis nostra aetate obtinet. Attamen haud raro sensus qui huiusmodi locutionibus in linguis hodiernis attribuitur, notionem alicuius varietatis seu discrepationis respectu habito ad textum primigenium eiusque significationem prae se fert. Ad omnem ambiguitatem excludendam, hac in Instructione, qua explicite de eodem argumento tractatur, adhibetur praesertim vocabulum «translatio» cum verbis ipsi cognatis. Etiamsi usurpatio eorundem durior quoad stylum latinitatis evadit aut de sic dicto «neologismo» redolet, hae locutiones indole quadam internationali gaudent, atque mentem Sedis Apostolicae in nostra aetate communicare faciliusque in multas linguas sine erroris periculo excipi possunt.

3   Cf. S. CONGR. PRO CULT. DIV., Ep. ad Praesides Conferentiarum Episcoporum «*Delinguis vulgaribus in S. Liturgiam inducendis*», diei 5 iunii 1976: *Notitiae* 12 (1976) 300-302.

2. Thereupon there began, under the care of the Supreme Pontiffs, the great work of renewal of the liturgical books of the Roman Rite, a work which included their translation[2] into vernacular languages, with the purpose of bringing about in the most diligent way that renewal of the sacred Liturgy which was one of the foremost intentions of the Council.

3. The liturgical renewal thus far has seen positive results, achieved through the labor and the skill of many, but in particular of the Bishops, to whose care and zeal this great and difficult duty is entrusted. Even so, the greatest prudence and care is required in the preparation of liturgical books marked by sound doctrine, which are exact in wording, free from all ideological influence, and otherwise endowed with those qualities by which the sacred mysteries of salvation and the indefectible faith of the Church are efficaciously transmitted by means of human language into prayer, and worthy worship is offered to God the Most High.[3]

2　The notion of the act of rendering a given text into another language is often expressed in Latin by the words *versio, conversio, interpretatio, redditio,* and even *mutatio, transductio* or similar words. Such is also the case in the Constitution *Sacrosanctum Concilium* and many other recent documents of the Holy See. Nevertheless, the sense often attributed to these terms in modern languages involves some variation or discrepancy from the original text and its meaning. For the purpose of excluding any ambiguity in this Instruction, which treats explicitly of the same theme, the word *translatio,* with its cognates, has been preferred. Even if their use presents some difficulty as regards Latin style or is redolent of a "neologism," such terms nevertheless have a certain international character and are able to communicate the present intent of the Apostolic See, as they are able to be employed in many languages without the danger of error.

3　Cf. S. Congr. for Divine Worship, Letter to the Presidents of the Conferences of Bishops *De linguis vulgaribus in S. Liturgiam inducendis,* 5 June 1976: *Notitiae* 12 (1976) 300-302.

4. Concilium Oecumenicum Vaticanum Secundum in deliberationibus ac decretis singulare momentum tribuit ritibus liturgicis, traditionibus ecclesiasticis ac disciplinae vitae christianae, propriis illarum Ecclesiarum particularium, praesertim Orientalium, quae veneranda antiquitate sunt praeclarae quaeque propterea variis modis traditionem declarant per Patres ab Apostolis acceptam.[4] Concilium expetivit, ut traditiones uniuscuiusque ex his Ecclesiis particularibus integrae et intactae servarentur; itaque, postulans ut varii Ritus secundum sanam traditionem recognoscerentur, principium statuit, ex quo solum eae mutationes inducerentur, quibus proprius et organicus progressus foveretur.[5] Eadem vigil cura sane requiritur ad tuendos et authentica ratione provehendos ritus liturgicos, traditiones ecclesiasticas atque disciplinam Ecclesiae Latinae, specialiter Ritus romani. Eadem cura etiam adhiberi debet operi transferendi in linguas populares textus liturgicos, praesertim Missale Romanum, quod haberi pergat praestantissimum signum et instrumentum integritatis et unitatis Ritus romani.[6]

---

4 Cf. CONC. OECUM. VAT. II, Decr. de Ecclesiis Orientalibus Catholicis *Orientalium Ecclesiarum*, n. 1.

5 Cf. CONC. OECUM. VAT. II, Const. *Sacrosanctum Concilium*, n. 4; Decr. *Orientalium Ecclesiarum*, nn. 2, 6.

6 Cf. CONC. OECUM. VAT. II, Const. *Sacrosanctum Concilium*, n. 38; PAULUS PP. VI, Const. Ap. *Missale Romanum*: AAS 61 (1969) 217-222. Cf. MISSALE ROMANUM, editio typica tertia: *Institutio Generalis*, n. 399.

4. The Second Vatican Ecumenical Council in its delibera-
tions and decrees assigned a singular importance to the liturgical rites, the ecclesiastical traditions, and the discipline of
Christian life proper to those particular Churches, especially
of the East, which are distinguished by their venerable antiq-
uity, manifesting in various ways the tradition received
through the Fathers from the Apostles.[4] The Council asked
that the traditions of each of these particular Churches be
preserved whole and intact. For this reason, even while
calling for the revision of the various Rites in accordance
with sound tradition, the Council set forth the principle that
only those changes were to be introduced which would foster
their specific organic development.[5] Clearly, the same vigilance is required for the safeguarding and the authentic
development of the liturgical rites, the ecclesiastical traditions, and the discipline of the Latin Church, and in particular, of the Roman Rite. The same care must be brought
also to the translation of the liturgical texts into vernacular
languages. This is especially true as regards the Roman
Missal, which will thus continue to be maintained as an
outstanding sign and instrument of the integrity and unity
of the Roman Rite.[6]

---

4   Cf. Second Vatican Council, Decr. On Eastern Catholic Churches, *Orientalium Ecclesiarum*,
    n. 1.

5   Cf. Second Vatican Council, Const. *Sacrosanctum Concilium*, n. 4; Decr. *Orientalium
    Ecclesiarum*, nn. 2, 6.

6   Cf. Second Vatican Council, Const. *Sacrosanctum Concilium*, n. 38; Pope Paul VI, Apost.
    Const. *Missale Romanum*: AAS 61 (1969) 217-222. Cf. Missale Romanum, editio typica
    tertia: *Institutio Generalis*, n. 399.

5. Re quidem vera licet affirmari ipsum Ritum romanum iam esse praetiosum exemplum et instrumentum verae inculturationis. Ritus enim romanus insignis est notabili facultate sibi assumendi textus, cantus, gestus et ritus a consuetudinibus atque ingenio diversarum gentium et Ecclesiarum particularium sive Orientis sive Occidentis deductos, ad aptam et convenientem unitatem, fines quarumvis regionum excedentem, efficiendam.[7] Haec proprietas praesertim est conspicua in eius orationibus, quae facultatem praebent primitivorum rerum adiunctorum limites superandi, ita ut orationes evadant christianorum cuiusvis loci atque aetatis. Ritus romani identitas atque expressio unitaria in praeparandis cunctis translationibus librorum liturgicorum summa diligentia sunt servandae,[8] non quasi quiddam mnemosynum historicum, sed ut manifestatio realitatum theologicarum communionis unitatisque ecclesialis.[9] Opus inculturationis, cuius rei translatio in linguas populares est pars, ideo ne habeatur quasi via ad nova genera vel familias rituum inferendas, contra, oportet

---

7   CONGR. DE CULT. DIV. ET DISC. SACR., Instr. IV «ad exsecutionem Constitutionis Concilii Vaticani II de sacra Liturgia recte ordinandam» *Varietates legitimae*, n. 17: AAS 87 (1995) 294-295; MISSALE ROMANUM, editio typica tertia: *Institutio Generalis*, n. 397.

8   CONC. OECUM. VAT. II, Const. *Sacrosanctum Concilium*, n. 38; MISSALE ROMANUM, editio typica tertia: *Institutio Generalis*, n. 397.

9   PAULUS PP. VI, Allocutio ad Consilium «ad exsequendam Constitutionem de S. Liturgia», diei 14 octobris 1968: AAS 60 (1968) 736.

5. Indeed, it may be affirmed that the Roman Rite is itself already a precious example and an instrument of true inculturation. For the Roman Rite is marked by a signal capacity for assimilating into itself spoken and sung texts, gestures and rites derived from the customs and the genius of diverse nations and particular Churches—both Eastern and Western—into a harmonious unity that transcends the boundaries of any single region.[7] This characteristic is particularly evident in its orations, which exhibit a capacity to transcend the limits of their original situation so as to become the prayers of Christians in any time or place. In preparing all translations of the liturgical books, the greatest care is to be taken to maintain the identity and unitary expression of the Roman Rite,[8] not as a sort of historical monument, but rather as a manifestation of the theological realities of ecclesial communion and unity.[9] The work of inculturation, of which the translation into vernacular languages is a part, is not therefore to be considered an avenue for the creation of new varieties or families of rites; on the contrary, it should be recognized that any adaptations

---

7   Congr. for Divine Worship and the Discipline of the Sacraments, Instr. IV "for the right implementation of the Second Vatican Council's Constitution on the Sacred Liturgy," *Varietates legitimae*, n. 17: AAS 87 (1995) 294-295; Missale Romanum, editio typica tertia: *Institutio Generalis*, n. 397.

8   Second Vatican Council, Const. *Sacrosanctum Concilium*, n. 38; Missale Romanum, editio typica tertia: *Institutio Generalis*, n. 397.

9   Pope Paul VI, Address to the Consilium "for the implementation of the Constitution on the Sacred Liturgy," 14 October 1968: AAS 60 (1968) 736.

reputetur quasvis accommodationes, inductas ut
necessitatibus culturalibus aut pastoralibus occurratur,
partes esse Ritus romani, eidemque inde harmonice
inserendas.[10]

6. Ex quo Constitutio de sacra Liturgia est promulgata,
opus, a Sede Apostolica promotum, pertinens ad
translationem textuum liturgicorum in linguas populares,
secum ferebat etiam emanationem normarum et consilia
Episcopis transmissa. Attamen perspectum est translationes
textuum liturgicorum variis in locis indigere mutatione in
melius per emendationem vel per novam redactionem.[11]
Omissiones aut errores, quibus quaedam translationes in
linguas populares usque adhuc sunt affectae, impediverunt
reapse debitam inculturationis progressionem, maxime quod
ad quasdam attinet linguas; unde factum est ut Ecclesiae
praecluderetur capacitas fundamenta iaciendi plenioris,
sanioris, veriorisque instaurationis.

7. Quapropter nunc necesse esse videtur nova ratione,
maturiore experientia iuvante, exponere principia
translationis, quibus inhaerendum erit cum in futuris
translationibus ex novo conficiendis tum in emendatione

---

10 Cf. CONGR. DE CULT. DIV. ET DISC. SACR., Instr. *Varietates legitimae*, n. 36: AAS 87 (1995)
302; cf. etiam Missale Romanum, editio typica tertia: *Institutio Generalis*, n. 398.

11 Cf. IOANNES PAULUS PP. II, Litt. Ap. *Vicesimus quintus annus*, diei 4 decembris 1988, n. 20:
AAS 81 (1989) 916.

introduced out of cultural or pastoral necessity become part
of the Roman Rite, and are thus to be inserted into it in a
harmonious way.[10]

6. Ever since the promulgation of the Constitution on the
Sacred Liturgy, the work of the translation of the liturgical texts into vernacular languages, as promoted by the
Apostolic See, has involved the publication of norms and
the communication to the Bishops of advice on the matter.
Nevertheless, it has been noted that translations of liturgical texts in various localities stand in need of improvement
through correction or through a new draft.[11] The omissions
or errors which affect certain existing vernacular translations—especially in the case of certain languages—have
impeded the progress of the inculturation that actually
should have taken place. Consequently, the Church has
been prevented from laying the foundation for a fuller,
healthier and more authentic renewal.

7. For these reasons, it now seems necessary to set forth anew,
and in light of the maturing of experience, the principles of
translation to be followed in future translations—whether
they be entirely new undertakings or emendations of texts

---

10 Cf. Congr. for Divine Worship and the Discipline of the Sacraments, Instr. *Varietates
legitimae*, n. 36: AAS 87 (1995) 302; cf. also Missale Romanum, editio typica tertia:
Institutio Generalis, n. 398.

11 Cf. Pope John Paul II, Apost. Letter *Vicesimus quintus annus*, 4 December 1988, n. 20:
AAS 81 (1989) 916.

textuum iam in usum inductorum, atque normas quasdam iam vulgatas distinctius definire, ratione habita plurium quaestionum ac rerum adiunctorum temporibus nostris exortarum. Ut plenus usus fiat experientiae, inde a celebrato Concilio haustae, videtur ad rem valere, si normae illae interdum ut propensiones enuntientur, quae in praeteritis translationibus perspicuae quaeque in futuris vitandae sunt. Reapse necessarium esse videtur ut vera notio translationis liturgicae iterum perpendatur, ita ut translationes sacrae Liturgiae in linguas populares sint securae ut vox authentica Ecclesiae Dei.[12] Haec ergo Instructio providet et parare studet novam aetatem instaurationis, quae indoli et traditioni Ecclesiarum particularium sit consentanea, sed etiam in tuto collocet fidem et unitatem universae Ecclesiae Dei.

8. Ea, quae in hac praesenti Instructione statuuntur, substituantur pro omnibus normis de eadem re antehac editis, excepta Instructione, *«Varietates legitimae»*, a Congregatione de Cultu Divino et Disciplina Sacramentorum die 25 mensis ianuarii 1994 publici iuris facta, cum qua Instructione novae hae normae componendae esse reputentur.[13] Normas, quae hac praesenti Instructione contineantur, iudicetur ad

---

12 Cf. Paulus PP. VI, Allocutioiis habita qui operam dant liturgicis textibus in vulgares linguas convertendis, diei 10 novembris 1965: AAS 57 (1965) 968.

13 Congr. de Cult. Div. et Disc. Sacr., Instr. *Varietates legitimae:* AAS 87 (1995) 288-314.

already in use—and to specify more clearly certain norms that have already been published, taking into account a number of questions and circumstances that have arisen in our own day. In order to take full advantage of the experience gained since the Council, it seems useful to express these norms from time to time in terms of tendencies that have been evident in past translations, but which are to be avoided in future ones. In fact, it seems necessary to consider anew the true notion of liturgical translation in order that the translations of the Sacred Liturgy into the vernacular languages may stand secure as the authentic voice of the Church of God.[12] This Instruction therefore envisions and seeks to prepare for a new era of liturgical renewal, which is consonant with the qualities and the traditions of the particular Churches, but which safeguards also the faith and the unity of the whole Church of God.

8. The norms set forth in this Instruction are to be substituted for all norms previously published on the matter, with the exception of the Instruction *Varietates legitimae*, published by the Congregation for Divine Worship and the Discipline of the Sacraments on 25 January 1994, in conjunction with which the norms in this present Instruction are to be understood.[13] The norms contained in this Instruction are to be

---

12 Cf. Pope Paul VI, Address to translators of liturgical texts into vernacular languages, 10 November 1965: AAS 57 (1965) 968.

13 Congr. for Divine Worship and the Discipline of the Sacraments, Instr. *Varietates legitimae*: AAS 87 (1995) 288-314.

translationem pertinere textuum usui liturgico destinatorum in Ritu romano, et, mutatis mutandis, in ceteris Ritibus Ecclesiae Latinae iure recognitis.

9. Ubi Congregationi de Cultu Divino et Disciplina Sacramentorum visum fuerit, exarabitur, collatis consiliis cum Episcopis, quibus interest, textus «ratio translationis» nuncupandus, auctoritate eiusdem Dicasterii definiendus, quo principia translationis in hac Instructione exposita ad certam quandam linguam pressius applicentur. Documentum illud, pro opportunitate, variis ex elementis constare potest, ex. gr., elencho vocabulorum popularium cum aliis latinis aequiparandorum, expositione principiorum specialiter ad determinatam linguam spectantium, et cetera.

I. De Eligendis Linguis Popularibus in Usum Liturgicum Introducendis

10. Primum perpendendum est de selectione linguarum, quas usurpari in liturgicis celebrationibus liceat. Opportunum est enim ut in unoquoque territorio ratio pastoralis elaboretur, quae respectum habeat praecipuorum idiomatum ibi exstantium, distinguendo inter sermones, quibus populus sponte loquitur, et eos, qui, cum non attingant naturalem communicationem ad mensuram rei pastoralis, maneant tantum res culturali studio proposito. In ratione illa concipienda et efficienda debite caveatur ne per electionem

considered applicable to the translation of texts intended for liturgical use in the Roman Rite and, *mutatis mutandis*, in the other duly recognized Rites of the Latin Church.

9. When it may be deemed appropriate by the Congregation for Divine Worship and the Discipline of the Sacraments, a text will be prepared after consultation with Bishops, called a *"ratio translationis,"* to be set forth by the authority of the same Dicastery, in which the principles of translation found in this Instruction will be applied in closer detail to a given language. This document may be composed of various elements as the situation may require, such as, for example, a list of vernacular words to be equated with their Latin counterparts, the setting forth of principles applicable specifically to a given language, and so forth.

I. On the Choice of Vernacular Languages to Be Introduced into Liturgical Use

10. To be considered first of all is the choice of the languages that it will be permissible to put into use in liturgical celebrations. Indeed, it is appropriate that there be elaborated in each territory a pastoral plan that takes account of the spoken languages there in use, with a distinction being made between languages which the people spontaneously speak and those which, not being used for ordinary communication in pastoral activity, merely remain the object of cultural interest. In considering and drafting such a plan, due caution

linguarum popularium in usum liturgicum introducendarum
fideles in parvas turmas secernantur, cum periculum sit
ne inter cives discordia foveatur in detrimentum unitatis
populorum, atque cum Ecclesiarum particularium tum
Ecclesiae universae.

11. In illa ratione etiam dilucide distinguatur ab hac
parte inter linguas, quae universe ad communicationem
pastoralem recipiantur, ab altera parte eas, quae in sacra
Liturgia adhibeantur. In ratione illa componenda oportet
item principium ducatur necessariorum adiumentorum,
quibus usus certi cuiusdem sermonis innitatur, sicut
numerus sacerdotum, diaconorum et collaboratorum
laicorum, qui sermone illo uti valeant, necnon numerus
hominum peritorum, exercitatorum et facultatem habentium
translationes omnium librorum liturgicorum Ritus romani
cum principiis hic enuntiatiis congruentes praeparandi;
necnon subsidiorum nummariorum ac technicorum ad
translationes conficiendas et libros typis imprimendos,
usu liturgico vere idoneos.

12. Necessaria insuper evadit distinctio in ambitu liturgico
inter linguas et idiomata dialectalia. Peculiari ratione dialecti,
quae communem ingenii formationem academicam et
culturalem non fulciunt, ad plenum liturgicum usum recipi
nequeunt, quia deficiunt stabilitate et amplitudine, quae
necessaria sunt, ut sint sermones liturgici intra fines
latiores. Quoquo modo, numerus particularium linguarum

should be exercised lest the faithful be fragmented into small groups by means of the selection of vernacular languages to be introduced into liturgical use, with the consequent danger of fomenting civil discord, to the detriment of the unity of peoples as well as of the unity of the particular Churches and the universal Church.

11. In this plan, a clear distinction is to be made also between those languages, on the one hand, that are used universally in the territory for pastoral communication, and those, on the other hand, that are to be used in the Sacred Liturgy. In drawing up the plan, it will be necessary to take account also of the question of the resources necessary for supporting the use of a given language, such as the number of priests, deacons and lay collaborators capable of using the language, in addition to the number of experts and those trained for and capable of preparing translations of all of the liturgical books of the Roman Rite in accord with the principles enunciated here. Also to be considered are the financial and technical resources necessary for preparing translations and printing books truly worthy of liturgical use.

12. Within the liturgical sphere, moreover, a distinction necessarily arises between languages and dialects. In particular, dialects that do not support common academic and cultural formation cannot be taken into full liturgical use, since they lack that stability and breadth that would be required for their being liturgical languages on a broader scale. In any event, the number of individual liturgical

liturgicarum ne nimis augeatur.[14] Hoc necesse est, ut in liturgicis celebrationibus intra confinia eiusdem nationis unitas quaedam sermonis foveatur.

13. Sermo autem, in plenum usum liturgicum non introductus, hac de causa non omnino ex ambitu liturgico excluditur. Adhiberi potest, saltem occasione data, in Oratione fidelium, in textibus cum cantu proferendis, in monitionibus aut partibus homiliae, praesertim si agitur de sermone christifidelium participum proprio. Manet tamen semper possibilitas linguam sive latinam sive aliam in eadem natione valde diffusam adhibendi, etiamsi sit sermo neque omnium neque maioris partis christifidelium hic et nunc celebrationis liturgicae participantium, dummodo discordia inter fideles vitetur.

14. Quoniam usurpatio linguarum in usum liturgicum, ex parte Ecclesiae effecta, in ipsius linguae progressionem incidere, immo eam determinare possunt, curandum est, ut illae provehantur linguae, quae licet iis fortasse non sit longa traditio litteris mandata, usurpari posse videantur a personis maioris numeri. Dialectorum fragmentatio vitetur oportet, praesertim dum aliqua dialectus a forma vocali ad

---

14 S. CONGR. PRO SACR. ET CULT. DIV., Ep. ad Praesides Conf. Episc. «De linguis vulgaribus in S. Liturgiam inducendis», diei 5 iunii 1976: Notitiae 12 (1976) 300-301.

languages is not to be increased too greatly.[14] This latter is necessary so that a certain unity of language may be fostered within the boundaries of one and the same nation in liturgical celebrations.

13. Moreover, the fact that a language is not introduced into full liturgical use does not mean that it is thereby altogether excluded from the Liturgy. It may be used, at least occasionally, in the Prayer of the Faithful, in the sung texts, in the invitations or instructions given to the people, or in parts of the homily, especially if the language is proper to some of Christ's faithful who are in attendance. Nevertheless, it is always possible to use either the Latin language or another language that is widely used in that country, even if perhaps it may not be the language of all—or even of a majority— of the Christian faithful taking part, provided that discord among the faithful be avoided.

14. Since the introduction of languages into liturgical use by the Church may actually affect the development of the language itself and may even be determinative in its regard, care is to be taken to promote those languages which—even while perhaps lacking a long literary tradition—seem capable of being employed by a greater number of persons. It is necessary to avoid any fragmentation of dialects, especially at the moment when a given dialect may be passing from spoken

---

14   S. Congr. for the Sacraments and Divine Worship, Letter to the Presidents of the
     Conferences of Bishops, De linguis vulgaribus in S. Liturgiam inducendis, 5 June 1976:
     Notitiae 12 (1976) 300-301.

scriptam transit. Auspicandum est semper, ex contra, ut formae loquendi communitatibus hominum communes foveantur seu promoveantur.

15. Conferentiae Episcoporum erit statuere quinam sermones in eius territorio vigentes in usum sive plenum sive partialem inducendi sunt. Quae statuta oportent a Sede Apostolica recognoscantur, antequam opus translationis quoquo modo inchoetur.[15] Priusquam sententiam hac de re ferat, Conferentia Episcoporum ne omittat mentem peritorum aliorumque operis sociorum per scripta colligere, quae vota, una cum ceteris actis, ad Congregationem de Cultu Divino et Disciplina Sacramentorum in scriptis mittantur, necnon una cum relatione, ut infra, ad art. 16.

16. Quod ad iudicium attinet Conferentiae Episcoporum, qua de inductione linguae popularis in usum liturgicum decernatur, haec, quae sequuntur, sunt observanda (cf. n. 79):[16]

---

15 Cf. CONC. OECUM. VAT. II, Const. *Sacrosanctum Concilium*, n. 36 §3; S. CONGR. PRO SACR. ET CULT. DIV., Ep. ad Praesides Conf. Episc. «*De linguis vulgaribus in S. Liturgiam inducendis*», diei 5 iunii 1976: *Notitiae* 12 (1976) 300-301.

16 Cf. CONC. OECUM. VAT. II, Const. *Sacrosanctum Concilium*, n. 36 §3; PAULUS PP. VI, Litt. Ap. *Sacram Liturgiam*, diei 25 ianuarii 1964: AAS 56 (1964) 143; S. RITUUM CONGR., Instr. *Inter Oecumenici*, diei 26 septembris 1964, nn. 27-29: AAS 56 (1964) 883; cf. S. CONGR. PRO SACR. ET CULT. DIV., Ep. ad Praesides Conf. Episc. «*De linguis vulgaribus in S. Liturgiam inducendis*», diei 5 iunii 1976: *Notitiae* 12 (1976) 300-302.

to written form. Instead, care should be taken to foster and to develop forms of speech that are common to human communities.

15. It will be the responsibility of the Conference of Bishops to determine which of the prevailing languages are to be introduced into full or partial liturgical use in its territory. The decisions of the Conference of Bishops require the *recognitio* of the Apostolic See before the work of translation is undertaken in any way.[15] Before giving its decision on this matter, the Conference of Bishops should not omit to seek the written opinion of experts and other collaborators in the work; these opinions, together with the other acts, are to be sent in written form to the Congregation for Divine Worship and the Discipline of the Sacraments, in addition to the *relatio* mentioned below, in art. n. 16.

16. As regards the decision of the Conference of Bishops for the introduction of a vernacular language into liturgical use, the following are to be observed (cf. n. 79):[16]

---

15 Cf. Second Vatican Council, Const. *Sacrosanctum Concilium*, n. 36 § 3; S. Congr. for the Sacraments and Divine Worship, Letter to the Presidents of the Conferences of Bishops *De linguis vulgaribus in S. Liturgiam inducendis*, 5 June 1976: *Notitiae* 12 (1976) 300-301.

16 Cf. Second Vatican Council, Const. *Sacrosanctum Concilium*, n. 36 § 3; Pope Paul VI, Apost. Letter *Sacram Liturgiam*, 25 January 1964: AAS 56 (1964) 143; S. Congr. of Rites, Inst. *Inter Oecumenici*, 26 September 1964, nn. 27-29: AAS 56 (1964) 883; cf. S. Congr. for the Sacraments and Divine Worship, letter to the Presidents of the Conferences of Bishops *De linguis vulgaribus in S. Liturgiam inducendis*, 5 June 1976: *Notitiae* 12 (1976) 300-302.

a. Ad legitima ferenda decreta, duae ex tribus suffragiorum secretorum partes requiruntur, ab omnibus iis qui in Conferentia Episcoporum iure fruuntur suffragium deliberativum ferendi;

b. Omnia acta ab Apostolica Sede probanda, in duplici exemplari exarata et a Praeside et Secretario Conferentiae et subscriptantur sigilloque debite muniantur, ad Congregationem de Cultu Divino et Disciplina Sacramentorum sunt transmittenda. Illis actis haec contineantur:

   i. nomina Episcoporum vel iure aequiparatorum, qui adunationi interfuerunt,

   ii. ratio de rebus actis, qua contineri debet exitus suffragationum, ad singula decreta pertinentium, addito numero faventium, adversantium et se suffragii latione abstinentium,

   iii. dilucida expositio singularum partium Liturgiae, quae in lingua vernacula proferri statuuntur;

a. For the legitimate passage of decrees, a two-thirds vote by secret ballot is required on the part of those in the Conference of Bishops who have the right to cast a deliberative vote;

b. All of the acts to be examined by the Apostolic See, prepared in duplicate, signed by the President and Secretary of the Conference and duly affixed with its seal, are to be sent to the Congregation for Divine Worship and the Discipline of the Sacraments. In these acts are to be contained the following:

    i. the names of the Bishops, or of those equivalent to them in law, who were present at the meeting,

    ii. a report of the proceedings, which should contain the outcome of the votes pertaining to the individual decrees, including the number of those in favor, the number opposed, and the number abstaining;

    iii. a clear exposition of the individual parts of the Liturgy into which the decision has been made to introduce the vernacular language;

c. In relatione peculiari, dilucide declaretur lingua, de qua agitur, necnon causae, quibus moventibus eiusmodi sermo in usum liturgicum ut introducendus sustinetur.

17. Circa usum linguarum «artificiosarum» qui interdum temporum decursu est propositus, textuum approbatio, necnon facultatis concessio, eos in actionibus liturgicis adhibendi, Sanctae Sedi stricte reservatur, quae facultas solummodo in peculiaribus rerum adiunctis atque pro bono pastorali fidelium tribuitur, collatis consiliis cum Episcopis quibus maius interest.[17]

18. In celebrationibus, quae aguntur pro gente alterius sermonis, sicut advenae, migrantes, peregrini, etc., licet, de consensu Episcopi dioecesani, sacram Liturgiam lingua populari celebrare eiusmodi hominibus nota, libro liturgico adhibito qui a compenti auctoritate iam sit approbatus atque a Sede Apostolica recognitus.[18] Quodsi eae celebrationes certis temporibus frequentius recurrunt, Episcopus dioecesanus brevem relationem ad Congregationem de Divino Cultu et Disciplina Sacramentorum mittat, in qua condiciones, numerum participantium et editiones adhibitas describantur.

---

17 Cf. ex. gr. CONGR.DE CULT. DIV. ET DISC. SACR., *Normae de celebranda Missa in «esperanto»*, diei 20 martii 1990: *Notitiae* 26 (1990) 693-694.

18 Cf. S. RITUUM CONGR., Instr. *Inter Oecumenici*, n. 41: AAS 56 (1964) 886.

c.   In a special report is to be included a clear explanation of
     the language involved, as well as the reasons for which the
     proposal has been made to introduce it into liturgical use.

17. As for the use of "artificial" languages, proposed from
time to time, the approval of texts as well as the granting
of permission for their use in liturgical celebrations is strictly
reserved to the Holy See. This faculty will be granted only
for particular circumstances and for the pastoral good of
the faithful, after consultation with the Bishops principally
involved.[17]

18. In celebrations for speakers of a foreign language, such
as visitors, migrants, pilgrims, etc., it is permissible, with the
consent of the diocesan Bishop, to celebrate the Sacred
Liturgy in a vernacular language known to these people,
using a liturgical book already approved by the competent
authority with the subsequent *recognitio* of the Apostolic
See.[18] If such celebrations recur with some frequency, the
diocesan Bishop is to send a brief report to the Congregation
for Divine Worship and the Discipline of the Sacraments,
describing the circumstances, the number of participants,
and the editions used.

---

17   Cf., for example, Congr. for Divine Worship and the Discipline of the Sacraments, *Normae
     de celebranda Missa in «esperanto»*, 20 March 1990: *Notitiae* 26 (1990) 693-694.

18   Cf. S. Congr. of Rites, Instr. *Inter Oecumenici*, n. 41: AAS 56 (1964) 886.

II. De Textuum Liturgicorum Translatione in Linguas Populares

1. Principia generalia cuivis translationi apta

19. Sacrae Scripturae verba necnon alia, quae dicta sunt in celebrationibus liturgicis, praesertim in celebrandis sacramentis, non in primis spectant, ut sint quasi speculum interioris dispositionis fidelium, sed veritates exprimunt, quae temporis ac loci fines exsuperant. Per haec enim verba Deus cum dilecti Filii sui Sponsa semper colloquitur, Spiritus Sanctus christifideles in omnem veritatem inducit verbumque Christi in eis abundanter inhabitare facit atque Ecclesia omne, quod ipsa est, et omne, quod credit, perpetuat atque transmittit, dum preces omnium fidelium ad Deum per Christum et in virtute Spiritus Sancti vertit.[19]

20. Textus liturgici latini Ritus romani, dum e saeculis experientiae ecclesialis in transmittenda fide Ecclesiae a Patribus accepta hauriunt, ipsi fructus sunt nuper allatus instaurationis liturgicae. Ut tantum patrimonium tantaeque divitiae serventur et per saecula transmittantur, ad principium in primis attendatur versionem textuum liturgicorum Liturgiae romanae opus esse non tam artificii

---

19 Cf. CONC. OECUM. VAT. II, Const. *Sacrosanctum Concilium*, n. 33; Const. Dogm. de divina Revelatione *Dei Verbum*, n. 8; cf. MISSALE ROMANUM, editio typica tertia: *Institutio Generalis*, n. 2.

II. On the Translation of Liturgical Texts into Vernacular Languages

1. General principles applicable to every translation

19. The words of the Sacred Scriptures, as well as the other words spoken in liturgical celebrations, especially in the celebration of the Sacraments, are not intended primarily to be a sort of mirror of the interior dispositions of the faithful; rather, they express truths that transcend the limits of time and space. Indeed, by means of these words God speaks continually with the Spouse of his beloved Son, the Holy Spirit leads the Christian faithful into all truth and causes the word of Christ to dwell abundantly within them, and the Church perpetuates and transmits all that she herself is and all that she believes, even as she offers the prayers of all the faithful to God, through Christ and in the power of the Holy Spirit.[19]

20. The Latin liturgical texts of the Roman Rite, while drawing on centuries of ecclesial experience in transmitting the faith of the Church received from the Fathers, are themselves the fruit of the liturgical renewal, just recently brought forth. In order that so great a patrimony of riches may be preserved and passed on through the centuries, it is to be kept in mind from the beginning that the translation of the liturgical texts of the Roman Liturgy is not so much a work

---

19 Cf. Second Vatican Council, Const. *Sacrosanctum Concilium*, n. 33; Dogm. Const. on Divine Revelation, *Dei Verbum*, n. 8; cf. Missale Romanum, editio typica tertia: *Institutio Generalis*, n. 2.

quam potius textus primigenios in linguam popularem fideliter et accurate reddendi. Licet debita concedatur facultas verba componendi atque syntaxim et stylum statuendi ad textum popularem profluentem et orationis popularis cursui idoneum exarandum, textus vero originalis seu primigenius oportet ut, quantum fieri potest, integerrime et peraccurate transferatur, nullis scilicet interpositis omissionibus vel additamentis, quoad argumentum rerum, nec paraphrasibus aut glossis inductis; accommodationes ad proprietates seu indolem variorum sermonum popularium oportet sint sobriae et caute efficiantur.[20]

21. In translationibus praesertim, quae populis recentius ad fidem Christi adductis destinantur, fidelitati et congruentiae cum sensu textus primigenii interdum opus est ut vocabula iam in usu communi nova ratione adhibeantur, verba vel locutiones novae condantur, voces textuum primigeniorum diverso scribendi modo reddantur vel aptentur pronuntiationi linguae popularis,[21] aut adhibeantur figurae sermonis quae ipsum sensum locutionis latinae integre exprimant, licet verbis aut syntaxi ab eadem differant. Huiusmodi consilia, praesertim cum de re maximi momenti agatur, exhibeantur deliberationi omnium Episcoporum, ad quos pertinet, antequam textui definitivo inserantur. Praeterea omni ex

---

20 Cf. CONSILIUM «AD EXSEQUENDAM CONSTITUTIONEM DE S. LITURGIA», Ep. ad Praesides Conf. Episc., diei 21 iunii 1967: *Notitiae* 3 (1967) 296; CARD. SECR. STATUS, Litt. ad Pro-Praefectum Congr. de Cult. Div. et Disc. Sacr. datae, diei 1 februarii 1997.

21 Cf. CONGR. DE CULT. DIV. ET DISC. SACR., Instr. *Varietates legitimae*, diei 25 ianuarii 1994, n. 53: AAS 87 (1995) 308.

of creative innovation as it is of rendering the original texts faithfully and accurately into the vernacular language. While it is permissible to arrange the wording, the syntax and the style in such a way as to prepare a flowing vernacular text suitable to the rhythm of popular prayer, the original text, insofar as possible, must be translated integrally and in the most exact manner, without omissions or additions in terms of their content, and without paraphrases or glosses. Any adaptation to the characteristics or the nature of the various vernacular languages is to be sober and discreet.[20]

21. Especially in the translations intended for peoples recently brought to the Christian Faith, fidelity and exactness with respect to the original texts may themselves sometimes require that words already in current usage be employed in new ways, that new words or expressions be coined, that terms in the original text be transliterated or adapted to the pronunciation of the vernacular language,[21] or that figures of speech be used which convey in an integral manner the content of the Latin expression even while being verbally or syntactically different from it. Such measures, especially those of greater moment, are to be submitted to the discussion of all the Bishops involved before being inserted into the definitive

---

20 Cf. the Consilium "for the implementation of the Constitution on the Sacred Liturgy," Letter to the Presidents of the Conferences of Bishops, 21 June 1967: *Notitiae* 3 (1967) 296; Card. Secr. of State, Letter to the Pro-Prefect of the Congr. for Divine Worship and the Discipline of the Sacraments, 1 February 1997.

21 Cf. Congr. for Divine Worship and the Discipline of the Sacraments, Instr., *Varietates legitimae*, 25 January 1994, n. 53: AAS 87 (1995) 308.

parte explicentur in relatione, de qua infra ad n. 79. Peculiari ratione cautela adhibeatur in vocabulis inducendis, quae de religionibus ethnicis ducta sunt.[22]

22. Accommodationes textuum secundum articulos 37-40 Constitutionis *Sacrosanctum Concilium* considerentur ut veris necessitatibus culturalibus et pastoralibus respondentes, non ortae e mera voluntate novitatem aut varietatem assequendi, nec putentur modi editiones typicas emendandi aut earundem summam sententiarum theologicarum mutandi, sed normis et procedendi rationibus regantur, quae in praedicta Instructione *Varietates legitimae* continentur.[23] Quapropter translationes in linguam popularem librorum liturgicorum, quae recognitionis causa Congregationi de Cultu Divino et Disciplina Sacramentorum proponuntur, contineant, praeter ipsam translationem cum quibusvis accommodationibus explicite praescriptis in editionibus typicis, tantum aptationes seu mutationes, quae assensu iam gaudeant scripto eiusdem Dicasterii.

23. In translationibus textuum manu ecclesiastica compositorum, etsi eiusdem textus fontem quae inveniatur inspicere et ope subsidiorum ad historiam aliasque scientias pertinentium agere expedit, tamen semper ipse textus editionis typicae latinae transferendus est.

---

22   *Ibidem*, n. 39: AAS 87 (1995) 303.

23   *Ibidem*: AAS 87 (1995) 288-314; cf. Missale Romanum, editio typica tertia, *Institutio Generalis*, n. 397.

draft. Moreover, they should be explained thoroughly in the *relatio* mentioned below in no. 79. In particular, caution should be exercised in introducing words drawn from non-Christian religions.[22]

22. Adaptations of the texts according to articles 37-40 of the Constitution *Sacrosanctum Concilium* are to be considered on the basis of true cultural or pastoral necessity, and should not be proposed out of a mere desire for novelty or variety, nor as a way of supplementing or changing the theological content of the *editiones typicae*; rather, they are to be governed by the norms and procedures contained in the above-mentioned Instruction *Varietates legitimae*.[23] Accordingly, translations into vernacular languages that are sent to the Congregation for Divine Worship and the Discipline of the Sacraments for the *recognitio* are to contain, in addition to the translation itself and any adaptations foreseen explicitly in the *editiones typicae*, only adaptations or modifications for which prior written consent has been obtained from the same Dicastery.

23. In the translation of texts of ecclesiastical composition, while it is useful with the assistance of historical and other scientific tools to consult a source that may have been discovered for the same text, nevertheless it is always the text of the Latin *editio typica* itself that is to be translated.

---

22 *Ibid.*, n. 39: AAS 87 (1995) 303.

23 *Ibid.*: AAS 87 (1995) 288-314; cf. Missale Romanum, editio typica tertia, *Institutio Generalis*, n. 397.

Quotiescumque in textu biblico aut liturgico servantur vocabula sumpta de aliis linguis antiquis (ex. gr. verba «*Alleluia*» et «*Amen*», vocabula aramaica in Novo Testamento contenta, vocabula graeca de «*Trisagion*» sumpta, quae in *Improperiis* feriae VI in Passione Domini proferuntur, et «*Kyrie eleison*» Ordinis Missae, praeter multa nomina propria) deliberandum est an eadem in nova populari translatione conservanda sint, saltem inter alia possibiliter eligenda. Immo, diligens respectus textus primigenii interdum postulabit, ut hoc modo agatur.

24. Praeterea omnino non licet translationes fieri e translationibus iam in alias linguas peractis, cum immediate ex textibus originalibus oporteat eas deduci, scilicet, de latino, quod spectat ad textus liturgicos manu ecclesiastica compositos, de lingua hebraica, aramaica vel graeca, si casus fert, quod respicit ad textus Sacrarum Scripturarum. Item in exarandis translationibus Sacrorum Bibliorum ad usum liturgicum, pro more inspiciendus est ut subsidium textus Novae Vulgatae editionis a Sede Apostolica promulgatae, ad traditionem exegeticam servandam, quae peculiariter ad Liturgiam Latinam spectat, sicut alibi in hac Instructione est expositum.[24]

25. Ut ea, quae in textu originali continentur etiam fidelibus peculiari institutione intellectuali carentibus pateant et ab iis intellegantur, translationibus id sit proprium, ut quibusdam verbis exprimantur, ad intellegentiam accommodatis,

---

24 Cf. S. Rituum Congr., Instr. *Inter Oecumenici*, n. 40, a: AAS 56 (1964) 885.

Whenever the biblical or liturgical text preserves words taken from other ancient languages (as, for example, the words *Alleluia* and *Amen*, the Aramaic words contained in the New Testament, the Greek words drawn from the *Trisagion* which are recited in the *Improperia* of Good Friday, and the *Kyrie eleison* of the Order of Mass, as well as many proper names) consideration should be given to preserving the same words in the new vernacular translation, at least as one option among others. Indeed, a careful respect for the original text will sometimes require that this be done.

24. Furthermore, it is not permissible that the translations be produced from other translations already made into other languages; rather, the new translations must be made directly from the original texts, namely the Latin, as regards the texts of ecclesiastical composition, or the Hebrew, Aramaic, or Greek, as the case may be, as regards the texts of Sacred Scripture.[24] Furthermore, in the preparation of these translations for liturgical use, the *Nova Vulgata Editio*, promulgated by the Apostolic See, is normally to be consulted as an auxiliary tool, in a manner described elsewhere in this Instruction, in order to maintain the tradition of interpretation that is proper to the Latin Liturgy.

25. So that the content of the original texts may be evident and comprehensible even to the faithful who lack any specialized intellectual formation, the translations should be characterized by a kind of language which is easily understandable,

---

24   Cf. S. Congr. of Rites, Instr. *Inter Oecumenici*, n. 40a: AAS 56 (1964) 885.

quae tamen simul dignitatem, decorem atque accuratum argumentum doctrinale huiusmodi textuum servent.[25] Per verba laudis et adorationis, quae reverentiam et animum gratum fovent erga Dei maiestatem eiusque potentiam, misericordiam, atque naturam transcendentem, translationes fami ac siti Dei vivi congruent, quas populus aetatis nostrae experitur, dum simul ad dignitatem et pulchritudinem ipsius celebrationis liturgicae conferunt.[26]

26. Indoles textuum liturgicorum, utpote instrumentum potentissimum ad elementa fidei et morum christianorum in vita christifidelium inculcanda,[27] in translationibus omni cura est servanda. Item translatio textuum congruere debet cum sana doctrina.

27. Etiamsi vitanda sunt vocabula aut locutiones, quae, propter indolem suam nimis insuetam aut importunam, facilem impediunt intellegentiam, nihilominus textus liturgici oportet considerentur vox Ecclesiae orantis potius quam peculiarium coetuum aut singulorum hominum, ideoque immunes esse debent ab usu nimis obnoxie inhaerendi modis

---

25   Cf. PAULUS PP. VI, Allocutioiis habita qui operam dant liturgicis textibus in vulgares linguas convertendis, diei 10 novembris 1965: AAS 57 (1965) 968; CONGR. DE CULT. DIV. ET DISC. SACR., Instr. *Varietates legitimae*, n. 53: AAS 87 (1995) 308.

26   Cf. IOANNES PAULUS PP. II, Allocutioad quosdam Civitatum Americae Septemtionalis epis-copos in sacrorum liminum visitatione, diei 4 decembris 1993, n. 2: AAS 86 (1994) 755-756.

27   Cf. CONC. OECUM. VAT. II, Const. *Sacrosanctum Concilium*, n. 33.

yet which at the same time preserves these texts' dignity, beauty, and doctrinal precision.[25] By means of words of praise and adoration that foster reverence and gratitude in the face of God's majesty, his power, his mercy and his transcendent nature, the translations will respond to the hunger and thirst for the living God that is experienced by the people of our own time, while contributing also to the dignity and beauty of the liturgical celebration itself.[26]

26. The liturgical texts' character as a very powerful instrument for instilling in the lives of the Christian faithful the elements of faith and Christian morality,[27] is to be maintained in the translations with the utmost solicitude. The translation, furthermore, must always be in accord with sound doctrine.

27. Even if expressions should be avoided which hinder comprehension because of their excessively unusual or awkward nature, the liturgical texts should be considered as the voice of the Church at prayer, rather than of only particular congregations or individuals; thus, they should be free of an overly servile adherence to prevailing modes of

---

25 Cf. Pope Paul VI, Address to translators of liturgical texts into vernacular languages, 10 November 1965: AAS 57 (1965) 968; Congr. for Divine Worship and the Discipline of the Sacraments, Instr. *Varietates legitimae*, n. 53: AAS 87 (1995) 308.

26 Cf. Pope John Paul II, Address to a group of Bishops from the United States of America on their *Ad limina* visit, 4 December 1993, n. 2: AAS 86 (1994) 755-756.

27 Cf. Second Vatican Council, Const. *Sacrosanctum Concilium*, n. 33.

vigentium expressionum. Si vero vocabula aut locutiones aliquando in textibus liturgicis adhiberi possunt, quae a sermone usitato et cotidiano differunt, haud raro hoc ipso evenit, ut textus revera faciliores ut memoria teneantur et efficaciores in rebus supernis exprimendis exstent. Immo videtur observantiam principiorum in hac Instructione expositorum prodesse ad gradatim efficiendum in omni lingua vulgari stylum sacrum, qui et tamquam sermo proprie liturgicus agnoscatur. Item fieri potest ut certa quaedam ratio loquendi, quae aliquantulum obsoleta in cotidiano sermone habeatur, pergat in liturgico contextu servari. Similiter, in locis biblicis transferendis, ubi vocabula aut locutiones specie inelegantes continentur, vitandus est nisus inconsideratus hanc proprietatem abstergendi. Haec vero principia Liturgiam eximent necessitate revisionum frequentium, cum de diversis agatur exprimendi modis, qui e populi consuetudine abierunt.

28. Sacra Liturgia non solum hominis intellectum devincit, sed totam etiam personam, quae est "subiectum" plenae et consciae participationis in celebratione liturgica. Sinant igitur interpretes signa imaginesve textuum et actiones rituales per se loqui, neque nitantur nimis explicitum reddere id, quod in textu originali est implicitum. Eandem ob causam, prudenter caveatur, ne textus explanationis addantur, qui in editione typica absunt. Attendatur insuper, ut in editionibus popularibus saltem aliquot textus lingua latina exarati

expression. If indeed, in the liturgical texts, words or expressions are sometimes employed which differ somewhat from usual and everyday speech, it is often enough by virtue of this very fact that the texts become more truly memorable and more capable of expressing heavenly realities. Indeed, it will be seen that the observance of the principles set forth in this Instruction will contribute to the gradual development, in each vernacular, of a sacred style that will come to be recognized as proper to liturgical language. Thus it may happen that a certain manner of speech which has come to be considered somewhat obsolete in daily usage may continue to be maintained in the liturgical context. In translating biblical passages where seemingly inelegant words or expressions are used, a hasty tendency to sanitize this characteristic is likewise to be avoided. These principles, in fact, should free the Liturgy from the necessity of frequent revisions when modes of expression may have passed out of popular usage.

28. The Sacred Liturgy engages not only the intellect, but the whole person, who is the "subject" of full and conscious participation in the liturgical celebration. Translators should therefore allow the signs and images of the texts, as well as the ritual actions, to speak for themselves; they should not attempt to render too explicit that which is implicit in the original texts. For the same reason, the addition of explanatory texts not contained in the *editio typica* is to be prudently avoided. Consideration should also be given to including in the vernacular editions at least some texts in the Latin

serventur, praesertim de inaestimabili thesauro cantus gregoriani, quem Ecclesia ut Liturgiae romanae proprium agnoscit et qui ideo in actionibus liturgicis, ceteris paribus, principem locum obtinere debet.[28] Cantus enim ille maxime valet ad spiritum humanum ad res supernas elevandum.

29. Homiliae et catechesis est textuum liturgicorum significationem exponere,[29] quae mentem Ecclesiae in lucem accurate ponat, quod spectat ad sodales Ecclesiarum particularium vel communitatum ecclesialium a plena communione cum Ecclesia Catholica seiunctarum, communitatum Iudaeorum aut ad sectatores aliarum religionum, necnon ad veram dignitatem et aequalitatem omnium hominum.[30] Similiter est catechistarum vel illius, qui homiliam habet, rectam interpretationem textuum transmittere, praeiudicio vel discrimine quovis iniusto destitutam quoad personas, genus, conditionem socialem,

---

28 Cf. *ibidem*, n. 116; S. RITUUM CONGR., Instr. *Musicam sacram*, diei 5 martii 1967, n. 50: AAS 59 (1967) 314; S. CONGR. PRO CULTO DIVINO, Ep. qua volumen «*Iubilate Deo*» ad Episcopos missum est, diei 14 aprilis 1974: *Notitiae* 10 (1974) 123-124; IOANNES PAULUS PP. II, Ep. *Dominicae Cenae*, diei 24 februarii 1980, n. 10: AAS 72 (1980) 135; Allocutio adquosdam Episcopos Conf. Civitat. Foederat. Americae Septentr. occasione oblata «*Ad limina Apostolorum*» coram admissos, diei 9 octobris 1998, n. 3: AAS 91 (1999) 353-354; cf. MISSALE ROMANUM, editio typica tertia, *Institutio Generalis*, n. 41.

29 Cf. CONC. OECUM. VAT. II, Const. *Sacrosanctum Concilium*, n. 35, 52; S. CONGR. RITUUM, Instr. *Inter Oecumenici*, n. 54: AAS 56 (1964) 890; cf. IOANNES PAULUS PP. II, Adh. Ap. *Catechesi tradendae*, diei 16 octobris 1979, n. 48: AAS 71 (1979) 1316. MISSALE ROMANUM, editio typica tertia: *Institutio Generalis*, n. 65.

30 Cf. CONC. OECUM. VAT. II, Decr. de Oecumenismo *Unitatis redintegratio*; Decl. de Ecclesiae habitudine ad Religiones non christianas *Nostra aetate*.

language, especially those from the priceless treasury of Gregorian chant, which the Church recognizes as proper to the Roman Liturgy, and which, all other things being equal, is to be given pride of place in liturgical celebrations.[28] Such chant, indeed, has a great power to lift the human spirit to heavenly realities.

29. It is the task of the homily and of catechesis to set forth the meaning of the liturgical texts,[29] illuminating with precision the mind of the Church regarding the members of particular Churches or ecclesial communities separated from full communion with the Catholic Church and those of Jewish communities, as well as adherents of other religions—and likewise, her understanding of the dignity and equality of all men.[30] Similarly, it is the task of catechists or of the homilist to transmit that right interpretation of the texts that excludes any prejudice or unjust discrimination on the basis of persons, gender, social condition, race or other criteria,

---

28 Cf. *ibid.*, n. 116; S. Congr. of Rites, Instr. *Musicam sacram*, 5 March 1967, n. 50: AAS 59 (1967) 314; S. Congr. for Divine Worship, Letter sent to the Bishops with the volume *Iubilate Deo*, 14 April 1974: *Notitiae* 10 (1974) 123-124; Pope John Paul II, Letter *Dominicae Cenae*, 24 February 1980, n. 10: AAS 72 (1980) 135; Address to a group of Bishops from the United States of America on their *Ad limina* visit, 9 October 1998, n. 3: AAS 91 (1999) 353-354; cf. Missale Romanum, editio typica tertia, *Institutio Generalis*, n. 41.

29 Cf. Second Vatican Council, Const. *Sacrosanctum Concilium*, n. 35, 52; S. Congr. of Rites, Instr. *Inter Oecumenici*, n. 54: AAS 56 (1964) 890; cf. Pope John Paul II, Apost. Exhortation *Catechesi tradendae*, 16 October 1979, n. 48: AAS 71 (1979) 1316; Missale Romanum, editio typica tertia: *Institutio Generalis*, n. 65.

30 Cf. Second Vatican Council, Decr. on Ecumenism, *Unitatis redintegratio*; Decl. on the Relationship of the Church to Non-Christian Religions, *Nostra aetate*.

stirpem vel alia, quae vero textibus sacrae Liturgiae minime insunt. Quamvis eiusmodi consideratio interdum iuvet, ut optetur inter varias translationes certae cuiusdam locutionis, tamen ne habeatur causa textum biblicum aut liturgicum rite promulgatum immutandi.

30. Multis in linguis nomina et pronomina habentur, quae unam eandem formam praebent coniunctim pro utroque genere, masculino et feminino. Instantia ut eiusmodi usus mutentur, non necessario habenda est tamquam effectus vel manifestatio germanae progressionis ipsius sermonis vigentis. Etiamsi necesse sit per catechesim caveatur, ut eiusmodi vocabula intellegi pergant hoc sensu «inclusivo», in ipsis translationibus tamen saepe fieri non potest, ut diversa vocabula adhibeantur sine detrimento subtilitatis in textu postulatae, influxus reciproci variorum eius verborum et locutionum eiusve concinnitatis. Exempli gratia, cum textus originalis utitur singulo vocabulo, nexum exprimenti inter singulum hominem et familiae vel communitatis humanae universitatem atque unitatem (sicut verbum hebraicum «*adam*», graecum «*anthropos*», latinum «*homo*»), haec ratio linguae textus primigenii servanda est in translatione. Quemadmodum aliis temporibus historiae accidit, Ecclesia ipsa libere statuere debet rationem linguae, quae maxime eius missioni doctrinali inserviat, neque decet eam subici normis glottologicis exterius iniunctis, quae huiusmodi missioni sint detrimento.

which has no foundation at all in the texts of the Sacred Liturgy. Although considerations such as these may sometimes help one in choosing among various translations of a certain expression, nevertheless they are not to be considered reasons for altering either a biblical text or a liturgical text that has been duly promulgated.

30. In many languages there exist nouns and pronouns denoting both genders, masculine and feminine, together in a single term. The insistence that such a usage should be changed is not necessarily to be regarded as the effect or the manifestation of an authentic development of the language as such. Even if it may be necessary by means of catechesis to ensure that such words continue to be understood in the "inclusive" sense just described, it may not be possible to employ different words in the translations themselves without detriment to the precise intended meaning of the text, the correlation of its various words or expressions, or its aesthetic qualities. When the original text, for example, employs a single term in expressing the interplay between the individual and the universality and unity of the human family or community (such as the Hebrew word 'adam, the Greek anthropos, or the Latin homo), this property of the language of the original text should be maintained in the translation. Just as has occurred at other times in history, the Church herself must freely decide upon the system of language that will serve her doctrinal mission most effectively, and should not be subject to externally imposed linguistic norms that are detrimental to that mission.

31. Singillatim: consilia systematice suscepta confugiendi ad improvidas solutiones sunt vitanda, sicut substitutio inconsiderata vocabulorum, commutatio a numero singulari ad pluralem, unicae vocis significationem collectivam exprimentis fractio in partes masculinam et femininam, aut inductio vocabulorum impersonalium vel abstractorum, quae omnia efficere possunt, ne proferatur idem sensus plenus alicuius verbi aut locutionis textus originalis. Huiusmodi solutiones periculum afferunt difficultates theologicas et anthropologicas in translationem inducendi. Hae sunt aliae normae peculiares:

a. Ubi de Deo omnipotenti vel de singulis personis Sanctissimae Trinitatis agitur, veritas traditionis atque statutus usus cuiusque linguae circa usum generis sunt servandi.

b. Cura specialis adhibeatur oportet eo consilio, ut vocabula coniuncta «Filius hominis» fideliter et diligenter reddantur. Magnum momentum christologicum et typologicum huius locutionis postulat etiam, ut per totam translationem regula sermonis adhibeatur, quae praestet haec vocabula coniuncta comprehendi posse in contextu totius translationis.

c. Vocabulum «patres», quod multis in locis biblicis et in textibus liturgicis manu ecclesiastica compositis invenitur, reddatur congruenti vocabulo masculino in linguas vernaculas, prout in contextu existimatur illud

31. In particular: to be avoided is the systematic resort to imprudent solutions such as a mechanical substitution of words, the transition from the singular to the plural, the splitting of a unitary collective term into masculine and feminine parts, or the introduction of impersonal or abstract words, all of which may impede the communication of the true and integral sense of a word or an expression in the original text. Such measures introduce theological and anthropological problems into the translation. Some particular norms are the following:

a. In referring to almighty God or the individual persons of the Most Holy Trinity, the truth of tradition as well as the established gender usage of each respective language are to be maintained.

b. Particular care is to be taken to ensure that the fixed expression "Son of Man" be rendered faithfully and exactly. The great Christological and typological significance of this expression requires that there should also be employed throughout the translation a rule of language that will ensure that the fixed expression remain comprehensible in the context of the whole translation.

c. The term "fathers," found in many biblical passages and liturgical texts of ecclesiastical composition, is to be rendered by the corresponding masculine word into vernacular languages insofar as it may be seen to refer

referri sive ad Patriarchas aut reges populi electi in
Vetere Testamento sive ad Patres Ecclesiae.

d. Quantum fieri potest in certa aliqua lingua populari,
usus pronominis feminini potius quam neutri servandus
est, si ad Ecclesiam refertur.

e. Vocabula propinquitatem familiarem aut alias relationes
significantia, veluti «frater», «soror», etc., quae dilucide
sunt aut masculina aut feminina pro contextu,
observentur in translatione.

f. Genus grammaticum angelorum, daemonum et
paganorum deorum dearumque secundum textum
originalem in lingua populari servetur, quantum
fieri potest.

g. In cunctis hisce rebus necesse est mens attendat ad
principia, quae supra sunt exposita ad nn. 27 et 29.

32. Non licet translationem textus primigenii plenam
significationem arctioribus finibus circumscribere.
Vitandae sunt propterea locutiones propriae praeconiorum
negotiatoriorum aut consiliorum vel inceptorum politicorum
et ideologicorum, modorum caducorum vel obnoxiorum
regionalibus idiomatibus vel ambiguitatibus significationis.
Enchiridia scholarum ad stylum pertinentia vel similia opera,
cum his proclivitatibus nonnumquam indulgent, nequeunt
haberi exemplaria pro translatione liturgica. Opera autem,

to the Patriarchs or the kings of the chosen people in the Old Testament, or to the Fathers of the Church.

d. Insofar as possible in a given vernacular language, the use of the feminine pronoun, rather than the neuter, is to be maintained in referring to the Church.

e. Words which express consanguinity or other important types of relationship, such as "brother," "sister," etc., which are clearly masculine or feminine by virtue of the context, are to be maintained as such in the translation.

f. The grammatical gender of angels, demons, and pagan gods or goddesses, according to the original texts, is to be maintained in the vernacular language insofar as possible.

g. In all these matters it will be necessary to remain attentive to the principles set forth above, in nn. 27 and 29.

32. The translation should not restrict the full sense of the original text within narrower limits. To be avoided on this account are expressions characteristic of commercial publicity, political or ideological programs, passing fashions, and those which are subject to regional variations or ambiguities in meaning. Academic style manuals or similar works, since they sometimes give way to such tendencies, are not to be considered standards for liturgical translation. On the other

quae communi ratione putantur «classica» in unaquaque lingua populari, utilia esse possunt ad proprium exemplar idoneum quoad vocabula et usum.

33. Usus litterarum uncialium in textibus liturgicis editionis typicae latinae necnon in translatione liturgica Sacrorum Bibliorum—sive honoris titulo sive alio modo cuiusdam momenti quoad sensum theologicum—in lingua populari retineatur, prout saltem structura alicuius linguae id fieri posse concedat.

2. Aliae normae ad versiones Sacrorum Bibliorum et ad praeparationem Lectionariorum pertinentes
34. Potius optandum est versionem Sacrarum Scripturarum parare, servatis principiis sanae exegesis atque exquisitae rationis litteratorum, qua autem diligenter attendatur ad postulata peculiaria usus liturgici, quod spectat ad stylum, verborum electio, et optionem inter unam alteramve interpretationem.

35. Ubi eiusmodi versio Sacrorum Bibliorum in certam aliquam linguam non habetur, necesse erit adhibere versionem iam ante paratam, et translationem opportune mutare, ut apta sit usui in liturgico contextu, secundum principia in hac Instructione proposita.

36. Ut fideles possint saltem textus maxime significantes Sacrae Scripturae memoria tenere, quibus etiam in privatis

hand, works that are commonly considered "classics" in a given vernacular language may prove useful in providing a suitable standard for its vocabulary and usage.

33. The use of capitalization in the liturgical texts of the Latin *editiones typicae* as well as in the liturgical transla-tion of the Sacred Scriptures, for honorific or otherwise theologically significant reasons, is to be retained in the vernacular language at least insofar as the structure of a given language permits.

2. Other norms pertaining to the translation of the Sacred Scriptures and the preparation of Lectionaries

34. It is preferable that a version of the Sacred Scriptures be prepared in accordance with the principles of sound exege-sis and of high literary quality, but also with a view to the particular exigencies of liturgical use as regards style, the selection of words, and the selection from among different possible interpretations.

35. Wherever no such version of the Sacred Scriptures exists in a given language, it will be necessary to use a previously prepared version, while modifying the translation wherever appropriate so that it may be suitable for use in the liturgical context according to the principles set forth in this Instruction.

36. In order that the faithful may be able to commit to mem-ory at least the more important texts of the Sacred Scriptures

orationibus informentur, summi est momenti ut translatio
Sacrorum Bibliorum, usui liturgico destinata, quadam
uniformitate ac stabilitate sit praedita, ita ut in omni territorio
habeatur una tantum translatio approbata, quae in cunctis
partibus variorum librorum liturgicorum adhibeatur.
Huiusmodi stabilitas maxime est optanda in Sacrorum
Bibliorum translationibus quorum crebrior est usus, veluti
in Psalterio, quod est fundamentalis liber precum pro populo
christiano.[31] Conferentiae Episcoporum instanter animantur
ut pro territoriis suis prospiciant licentiae et editioni integrae
translationis Sacrarum Scripturarum, studio et lectioni
privatis fidelium destinatae, quae ex omni parte cum textu
in sacra Liturgia adhibito congruat.

37. Si translatio biblica, unde Lectionarium est compositum,
ostendit lectiones, quae ab illis in textu liturgico latino
propositis differunt, attendatur oportet omnia ad normam
Novae Vulgatae editionis esse referenda quoad textum
canonicum Sacrarum Scripturarum definiendum.[32] Ideo
in textibus deuterocanonicis et alibi, scilicet ubi sunt

---

31 Cf. PAULUS PP. VI, Const. Ap. *Laudis canticum*, diei 1 novembris 1970, n. 8: AAS 63
(1971) 532-533; OFFICIUM DIVINUM, Liturgia Horarum iuxta Ritum romanum, editio
typica altera 1985: *Institutio Generalis de Liturgia Horarum*, n. 100; IOANNES PAULUS PP. II,
Litt. Ap. *Vicesimus quintusannus*, n. 8: AAS 81 (1989) 904-905.

32 Cf. CONC. OECUM. TRID., Sessio IV, diei 8 aprilis 1546, *De libris sacris et de traditionibus
recipiendis*, et *De vulgata editione Bibliorum et de modo interpretandi s. Scripturam*: Denz.-
Schönm, nn. 1501-1508; IOANNES PAULUS PP. II, Const. Ap. *Scripturarum thesaurus*, diei
25 aprilis 1979: AAS 71 (1979) 558-559.

and be formed by them even in their private prayer, it is of the greatest importance that the translation of the Sacred Scriptures intended for liturgical use be characterized by a certain uniformity and stability, such that in every territory there should exist only one approved translation, which will be employed in all parts of the various liturgical books. This stability is especially to be desired in the translation of the Sacred Books of more frequent use, such as the Psalter, which is the fundamental prayer book of the Christian people.[31] The Conferences of Bishops are strongly encouraged to provide for the commissioning and publication in their territories of an integral translation of the Sacred Scriptures intended for the private study and reading of the faithful, which corresponds in every part to the text that is used in the Sacred Liturgy.

37. If the biblical translation from which the Lectionary is composed exhibits readings that differ from those set forth in the Latin liturgical text, it should be borne in mind that the *Nova Vulgata Editio* is the point of reference as regards the delineation of the canonical text.[32] Thus, in the translation of the deuterocanonical books and wherever else there may

---

31 Cf. Pope Paul VI, Apost. Const. *Laudis canticum*, 1 November 1970. n. 8: AAS 63 (1971) 532-533; Officium Divinum, Liturgia Horarum iuxta Ritum romanum, editio typica altera 1985: *Institutio Generalis de Liturgia Horarum*, n. 100; Pope John Paul II, Apost. Letter *Vicesimus quintus annus*, n. 8: AAS 81 (1989) 904-905.

32 Cf. Council of Trent, Session IV, 8 April 1546, *De libris sacris et de traditionibus recipiendis*, and *De vulgata editione Bibliorum et de modo interpretandi s. Scripturarum*: Denz.-Schönm., nn. 1501-1508; Pope John Paul II, Apost. Const. *Scripturarum thesaurus*, 25 April 1979: AAS 71 (1979) 558-559.

traditiones manu scriptae variae, translatio liturgica oportet iuxta eandem traditionem conficiatur, quam Nova Vulgata editio est secuta. Si translatio quaedam iam peracta optionem praebet contrariam iis, quae in Nova Vulgata editione redduntur, quod pertinet ad traditionem textualem subiacentem, ad ordinem versiculorum aut similia, remedium oportet afferatur in quovis Lectionario apparando, ita ut conformatio ad textum liturgicum latinum approbatum pergatur. In novis translationibus apparandis utile erit, licet sine obligatione, ut numeratio versiculorum quam arctissime hunc textum sequatur.

38. Saepe conceditur ut, de consensu editionum critica ratione vulgatarum et probantibus generatim peritis, lectio altera versiculi inducatur. Hoc autem non licet, ad textus liturgicos quod attinet, si de elementis lectionis agitur, quae momentum habent ob eorum convenientiam cum liturgico contextu, vel si principia in hac Instructione edita aliter in discrimen adducuntur. Circa locos hoc destitutos consensu critica ratione textus, peculiaris ratio ducatur earum optionum, quae textu approbato latino continentur.[33]

---

33 Cf. Paulus PP. VI, Allocutio ad Cardinales et ad Curiae Romanae Praelatos, diei 23 decembris 1966, n. 11: AAS 59 (1967) 53-54; cf. Allocutio ad Cardinales et ad Curiae Romanae Praelatos, diei 22 decembris 1977: AAS 70 (1978) 43; cf. Ioannes Paulus PP. II, Const. Ap. *Scripturarum thesaurus*, diei 25 aprilis 1979: AAS 71 (1979) 558; *Nova Vulgata Bibliorum Sacrorum*, editio typica altera 1986, Praefatio ad Lectorem.

exist varying manuscript traditions, the liturgical translation must be prepared in accordance with the same manuscript tradition that the *Nova Vulgata* has followed. If a previously prepared translation reflects a choice that departs from that which is found in the *Nova Vulgata Editio* as regards the underlying textual tradition, the order of verses, or similar factors, the discrepancy needs to be remedied in the preparation of any Lectionary so that conformity with the Latin liturgical text may be maintained. In preparing new translations, it would be helpful, though not obligatory, that the numbering of the verses also follow that of the same text as closely as possible.

38. It is often permissible that a variant reading of a verse be used, on the basis of critical editions and upon the recommendation of experts. However, this is not permissible in the case of a liturgical text where such a choice would affect those elements of the passage that are pertinent to its liturgical context, or whenever the principles found elsewhere in this Instruction would otherwise be neglected. For passages where a critical consensus is lacking, particular attention should be given to the choices reflected in the approved Latin text.[33]

---

33 Cf. Pope Paul VI, Address to the Cardinals and Prelates of the Roman Curia, 23 December 1966, n. 11: AAS 59 (1967) 53-54; cf. Address to the Cardinals and Prelates of the Roman Curia, 22 December 1977: AAS 70 (1978) 43; cf. Pope John Paul II, Apost. Const. *Scripturarum thesaurus*, 25 April 1979: AAS 71 (1979) 558; *Nova Vulgata Bibliorum Sacrorum*, editio typica altera 1986, Praefatio ad Lectorem.

39. Circumscriptio pericoparum biblicarum omnino conformetur ad Ordinem lectionum Missae vel ad alios textus liturgicos approbatos et recognitos, ut casus fert.

40. Servatis postulatis sanae exegesis, omnis cura adhibeatur, ut verba sententiarum biblicarum communiter usitarum in catechesi et in orationibus devotionem popularem exprimentibus retineantur. Ex altera parte summa ope nitendum est, ne corpus verborum aut stylus recipiantur, quae populus catholicus facile confundat cum loquendi consuetudine communitatum ecclesialium non catholicarum, aut aliarum religionum, ne inde confusio oriatur vel molestia afferatur.

41. Opera detur, ut translationes ad intellectum locorum biblicorum ab usu liturgico ac traditione Patrum Ecclesiae transmissum conformentur, praesertim cum de textibus magni momenti agitur, sicut psalmi et lectiones in praecipuis celebrationibus anni liturgici adhibitae; his in casibus diligentissime curetur oportet, ut translatio traditum sensum christologicum, typologicum aut spiritualem exprimat atque unitatem et nexum inter utrumque Testamentum manifestet.[34] Quapropter:

a. expedit ut Novae Vulgatae editioni inhaereatur, cum necesse sit decernere inter varias rationes, quae possunt

---

34 Cf. Officium Divinum, Liturgia Horarum iuxta Ritum romanum, editio typica altera 1985: *Institutio Generalis de Liturgia Horarum*, nn. 100-109.

39. The delineation of the biblical *pericopai* is to conform entirely to the *Ordo lectionum Missae* or to the other approved and confirmed liturgical texts, as the case may be.

40. With due regard for the requirements of sound exegesis, all care is to be taken to ensure that the words of the biblical passages commonly used in catechesis and in popular devotional prayers be maintained. On the other hand, great caution is to be taken to avoid a wording or style that the Catholic faithful would confuse with the manner of speech of non-Catholic ecclesial communities or of other religions, so that such a factor will not cause them confusion or anxiety.

41. The effort should be made to ensure that the translations be conformed to that understanding of biblical passages which has been handed down by liturgical use and by the tradition of the Fathers of the Church, especially as regards very important texts such as the Psalms and the readings used for the principal celebrations of the liturgical year; in these cases the greatest care is to be taken so that the translation express the traditional Christological, typological and spiritual sense, and manifest the unity and the inter-relatedness of both Testaments.[34] For this reason:

a. it is advantageous to be guided by the *Nova Vulgata Editio* wherever there is a need to choose, from among various possibilities [of translation], that one which is most suited

---

34 Cf. Officium Divinum, Liturgia Horarum iuxta Ritum romanum, editio typica altera 1985: *Institutio Generalis de Liturgia Horarum*, nn. 100-109.

haberi, maximam idoneam illam ad exprimendum modum, quo textus more tradito lectus est et receptus in traditione liturgica latina;

b. ad haec assequenda proposita referatur etiam ad antiquissimas versiones Sacrarum Scripturarum, velut graecam versionem Veteris Testamenti «a LXX viris» communiter nuncupatam, quae usui fuit christifidelibus inde a priscis Ecclesiae temporibus;[35]

c. iuxta traditionem ab immemorabili receptam, immo in supradicta versione «LXX virorum» iam perspicuam, nomen Dei omnipotentis, sacro tetragrammate hebraice expressum, latine vocabulo «Dominus», in quavis lingua populari vocabulo quodam eiusdem significationis reddatur.

Denique translatores instanter moneantur, ut attente perspiciant historiam interpretationis, quae hauriri potest e locis biblicis in scriptis Patrum Ecclesiae prolatis, vel etiam ex imaginibus biblicis crebrius in arte et hymnodia christiana praebitis.

42. Licet cavendum sit, ne historico contextui locorum biblicorum obscuritas afferatur, perpendat translator verbum Dei, in Liturgia nuntiatum, non esse ut documentum quoddam mere historicum. Textus enim biblicus non

---

35 Cf. CONC. VAT. II, Const. *Dei Verbum*, n. 22.

for expressing the manner in which a text has tradition-ally been read and received within the Latin liturgical tradition;

b. for the same purpose, other ancient versions of the Sacred Scriptures should also be consulted, such as the Greek version of the Old Testament commonly known as the "Septuagint," which has been used by the Christian faithful from the earliest days of the Church;[35]

c. in accordance with immemorial tradition, which indeed is already evident in the above-mentioned "Septuagint" version, the name of almighty God expressed by the sacred Hebrew *tetragrammaton* (YHWH) and rendered in Latin by the word *Dominus*, is to be rendered into any given vernacular by a word equivalent in meaning.

Finally, translators are strongly encouraged to pay close attention to the history of interpretation that may be drawn from citations of biblical texts in the writings of the Fathers of the Church, and also from those biblical images more frequently found in Christian art and hymnody.

42. While caution is advisable lest the historical context of the biblical passages be obscured, the translator should also bear in mind that the word of God proclaimed in the Liturgy is not simply an historical document. For the biblical text treats not only of the great persons and events of the Old

---

35   Second Vatican Council, Const. *Dei Verbum*, n. 22.

modo de praeclaris hominibus et eventis Veteris ac Novi Testamenti agit, sed de mysteriis quoque salutis, et ad fideles nostrae aetatis necnon ad eorum vitam repetit. Servata semper norma fidelitatis erga textum originalem, cum aliquod verbum vel locutio optionem praebet inter plures translationis rationes, quae fieri possunt, conetur, ut optio illa secum ferat auditorem seipsum ac lineamenta quaedam suae vitae in personis et eventibus in textu propositis quam vivide agnoscere.

43. Omnes formae quae caelitum imagines et gesta in humanam figuram fingunt vel denominationibus definitis seu «concretis» exprimunt, quod saepissime in sermone biblico evenit, modo nonnumquam vim suam servant, cum ad litteram vertuntur, velut in Novae Vulgatae editionis vocabula *«ambulare»*, *«brachium»*, *«digitus»*, *«manus»*, *«vultus»* Dei, *«caro»*, *«cornu»*, *«os»*, *«semen»*, *«visitare»*; quae vero potius est ne explanentur aut interpretata reddantur per voces vulgares magis «abstractas» vel vagas. Ad vocabula quaedam quod attinet, velut ea, quae *«anima»* et *«spiritus»* in Nova Vulgata transferuntur, cavendum est de principiis supra, ad nn. 40-41, expositis. Ideo vitandum est ut pro iis pronomen personale aut verbum magis «abstractum» potius habeatur, nisi hoc, aliquo in casu, stricte necessarium sit. Cogitetur enim translationem ad litteram factam locutionum, quae mirae animadvertantur in sermone vulgari, hanc ipsam ob rem audientis inquisitionem exposcere atque occasionem dare catechesis tradendae.

and New Testaments, but also of the mysteries of salvation, and thus refers to the faithful of the present age and to their lives. While always maintaining due regard for the norm of fidelity to the original text, one should strive, whenever there is a choice to be made between different ways of translating a term, to make those choices that will enable the hearer to recognize himself and the dimensions of his own life as vividly as possible in the persons and events found in the text.

43. Modes of speech by which heavenly realities and actions are depicted in human form, or designated by means of limited, concrete terminology—as happens quite frequently in biblical language (i.e., anthropomorphisms)—often maintain their full force only if translated somewhat literally, as in the case of words in the *Nova Vulgata Editio* such as *ambulare, brachium, digitus, manus,* or *vultus* [Dei], as well as *caro, cornu, os, semen,* and *visitare.* Thus it is best that such terms not be explained or interpreted by more abstract or general vernacular expressions. As regards certain terms, such as those translated in the *Nova Vulgata* as *anima* and *spiritus,* the principles mentioned in above nn. 40-41 should be observed. Therefore, one should avoid replacing these terms by a personal pronoun or a more abstract term, except when this is strictly necessary in a given case. It should be borne in mind that a literal translation of terms which may initially sound odd in a vernacular language may for this very reason provoke inquisitiveness in the hearer and provide an occasion for catechesis.

44. Ut aptior sit translatio in Liturgia enuntiari, necesse est vitetur omnis locutio ambigua auditu vel eo perplexa, ut audiens sensum rei amittat.

45. Praeter ea, quae in Praenotandis Ordinis lectionum Missae exponuntur, in biblico Lectionario vulgari sermone comparando ad postulata quae sequuntur attendatur:

a. Loci Sacrae Scripturae in Praenotandis allati omnino congruant cum translatione eorundem locorum in biblicis lectionibus, quae in Lectionario continentur.

b. Item tituli ad argumentum pertinentes, qui lectionibus praeponuntur, biblicam translationem in lectione adhibitam accurate retineant, si haec congruentia in Ordine lectionum Missae adest.

c. Item demum verba, prout in Ordine lectionum Missae praescripta, initio lectionis posita et «incipit» nuncupata, sequantur quam arctissime versionem biblicam in linguam vulgarem, unde de more sumpta sunt, neque aliis translationibus inhaereant. Quod vero ad huiusmodi elementa attinet, quae ipsius textus biblici non sunt, in Lectionariis componendis accurate vertantur ex latino in sermonem vulgarem, nisi

44. In order for a translation to be more easily proclaimed, it is necessary that any expression be avoided which is confusing or ambiguous when heard, such that the hearer would fail to grasp its meaning.

45. Apart from that which is set forth in *Praenotanda* of the *Ordo lectionum Missae*, the following norms are to be observed in the preparation of a Lectionary of biblical readings in a vernacular language:

a.   Passages of Sacred Scripture contained in the *Praenotanda* of the *Ordo lectionum Missae* are to conform completely to the translation of the same passages as they occur in the biblical readings within the Lectionary.

b.   Likewise the titles, expressing the theme of the readings and placed at the head of them, are to retain the wording of the readings themselves, wherever such a correspondence exists in the *Ordo lectionum Missae*.

c.   Finally, the words prescribed by the *Ordo lectionum Missae* for the beginning of the reading, called the *incipits*, are to follow as closely as possible the wording of the vernacular biblical version from which the readings are generally taken, refraining from following other translations. As regards those parts of the *incipits* that are not part of the biblical text itself, these are to be translated exactly from the Latin into the vernacular liturgies when preparing Lectionaries, unless the

Conferentia Episcoporum petierit et consecuta sit
praeviam licentiam Congregationis de Cultu Divino et
Disciplina Sacramentorum, qua concessum sit, ut alia
procedendi ratio in lectionum introitu haberetur.

3. Normae circa translationem ceterorum textuum liturgicorum

46. Normae supra statutae et eae, quae Sacram Scripturam
respiciunt, applicari debent, mutatis mutandis, textibus
quoque liturgicis ecclesiastica manu compositis.

47. Quoniam translatio thesaurum orationum oportet
transmittat perennem sermone quodam expressum, qui
scilicet intellegi possit in «contextu culturali», cui destinatur,
regatur etiam persuasione, qua vera precatio liturgica non
solum culturae ingenio formatur, sed ipsa ad efformandam
culturam confert, quapropter nihil mirum si aliquatenus
differre potest a sermocinatione communi. Translatio
liturgica, quae debitam auctoritatis atque integritatis sensus
textuum originalium rationem reddit, praestat, ut lingua sacra
vulgaris gignatur, cuius vocabula, syntaxis et grammatica
cultus divini propria sint, licet vero non praetermittant vim
et auctoritatem habere in sermonem cotidianum, sicut evenit
in linguas gentium antiquioris evangelizationis.

48. Textus praecipuarum festivitatum per annum liturgicum
occurrentium fidelibus praebeantur translatione, quae
facile memoria tenetur, ita ut etiam in privatis orationibus
possint adhiberi.

Conference of Bishops shall have sought and obtained the prior consent of the Congregation for Divine Worship and the Discipline of the Sacraments authorizing a different procedure for introducing the readings.

3. Norms concerning the translation of other liturgical texts

46. The norms set forth above, and those regarding Sacred Scripture, should also be applied, *mutatis mutandis*, to the texts of ecclesiastical composition.

47. While the translation must transmit the perennial treasury of orations by means of language understandable in the cultural context for which it is intended, it should also be guided by the conviction that liturgical prayer not only is formed by the genius of a culture, but itself contributes to the development of that culture. Consequently it should cause no surprise that such language differs somewhat from ordinary speech. Liturgical translation that takes due account of the authority and integral content of the original texts will facilitate the development of a sacral vernacular, characterized by a vocabulary, syntax and grammar that are proper to divine worship, even though it is not to be excluded that it may exercise an influence even on everyday speech, as has occurred in the languages of peoples evangelized long ago.

48. The texts for the principal celebrations occurring throughout the liturgical year should be offered to the faithful in a translation that is easily committed to memory, so as to render them usable in private prayers as well.

A. *De vocabulis*

49. Traditionis liturgicae romanae aliorumque catholicorum Rituum est, ut in eorum orationibus habeatur ratio per se cohaerens vocabulorum et eloquendi consuetudinum, libris Sacrae Scripturae et ecclesiali traditione sancitorum, potissimum autem scriptis Patrum Ecclesiae. Ratio ergo translationis librorum liturgicorum gerendae convenientiam faveat inter textum biblicum ipsum et textus liturgicos, manu ecclesiastica compositos, verbis biblicis aut de ipsis mentionem quandam saltem implicitam refertos.[36] In huiusmodi textibus expedit, ut translator dirigatur ratione eloquendi propria translationis Sacrarum Scripturarum iam approbatae pro usu liturgico in territoriis, in quorum utilitatem translatio efficitur. Eodem tempore cura impendatur, ne textus deprimatur, eo quod nimis insistitur in subtilioribus huiusmodi significationibus biblicis inhabiliter provehendis.

50. Cum libri liturgici Ritus romani multa contineant verba fundamentalia traditionis theologicae ac spiritualis Ecclesiae romanae, studeatur, ut horum vocabulorum ratio servetur, ne pro verbis alia substituantur, quae aliena sint ab usu liturgico et catechetico populi Dei in certo contextu culturali et ecclesiali. Quapropter haec principia specialiter sunt observanda:

---

36 Cf. PAULUS PP. VI, Adh. Ap. *Marialis cultus*, diei 11 februarii 1974, n. 30: AAS 66 (1974) 141-142.

A. Vocabulary

49. Characteristic of the orations of the Roman liturgical tradition as well as of the other Catholic Rites is a coherent system of words and patterns of speech, consecrated by the books of Sacred Scripture and by ecclesial tradition, especially the writings of the Fathers of the Church. For this reason the manner of translating the liturgical books should foster a correspondence between the biblical text itself and the liturgical texts of ecclesiastical composition which contain biblical words or allusions.[36] In the translation of such texts, the translator would best be guided by the manner of expression that is characteristic of the version of the Sacred Scriptures approved for liturgical use in the territories for which the translation is being prepared. At the same time, care should be taken to avoid weighting down the text by clumsily over-elaborating the more delicate biblical allusions.

50. Since the liturgical books of the Roman Rite contain many fundamental words of the theological and spiritual tradition of the Roman Church, every effort must be made to preserve this system of vocabulary rather than substituting other words that are alien to the liturgical and catechetical usage of the people of God in a given cultural and ecclesial context. For this reason, the following principles in particular are to be observed:

---

36 Cf. Pope Paul VI, Apost. Exhortation *Marialis cultus*, 11 February 1974, n. 30: AAS 66 (1974) 141-142.

a. In transferendis verbis rationem theologicam maxime significantibus, conveniens coordinatio quaeratur inter textum liturgicum et translationem in linguam vulgarem Catechismi Ecclesiae Catholicae auctoritate probatam, si eiusmodi translatio habetur aut componitur in linguam, de qua agitur, aut in linguam maxime affinem;

b. Item cum dedecet, ut idem vocabulum vel eadem locutio in textu liturgico servetur quam in Catechismo, translator curare debet, ut reddatur totus sensus doctrinalis ac theologicus, qui in vocabulis atque in integritate textus ipsius continetur;

c. Vocabula, quae progressu quodam sunt aptata in lingua aliqua vulgari, ut singuli liturgici ministri, vasa, supellectilia et vestes, distinguantur a personis rebusque similibus, ad vitam usumque cotidianam pertinentibus, serventur neque pro iis verba tali sacra indole carentia substituantur;

d. Constantia in transferendis vocabulis magni momenti servanda est per varias partes Liturgiae, ratione, ut decet, habita n. 53 infra positi.

51. Ceterum varietati vocabulorum in textu originali occurrenti respondeat, quantum fieri potest, varietas, qua translationes sint praeditae. Exempli gratia, usus eiusdem vocabuli vulgaris, quo variae formae verborum latinorum reddantur, sicut «satiari», «sumere», «vegetari» et «pasci»

a. In translating words of greater theological significance, an appropriate degree of coordination should be sought between the liturgical text and the authoritative vernacular translation of the *Catechism of the Catholic Church*, provided that such a translation exists or is being prepared, whether in the language in question or in a very closely related language;

b. Whenever it would be inappropriate to use the same vocabulary or the same expression in the liturgical text as in the *Catechism*, the translator should be solicitous to render fully the doctrinal and theological meaning of the terms and of the text itself as a whole;

c. One should maintain the vocabulary that has gradually developed in a given vernacular language to distinguish the individual liturgical ministers, vessels, furnishings, and vesture from similar persons or things pertaining to everyday life and usage; words that lack such a sacral character are not to be used instead;

d. In translating important words, due constancy is to be observed throughout the various parts of the Liturgy, with due regard for n. 53 below.

51. On the other hand, a variety of vocabulary in the original text should give rise, insofar as possible, to a corresponding variety in the translations. The translation may be weakened and made trite, for example, by the use of a single vernacular term for rendering differing Latin terms such as *satiari, sumere,*

ex una parte, aut nomina *«caritas»* ac *«dilectio»* ex altera, aut item vocabula *«anima»*, *«animus»*, *«cor»*, *«mens»* et *«spiritus»*, cum iterantur, textum potest extenuare ac tritum efficere. Item defectus in translatione variorum modorum Deum alloquendi, velut *«Domine»*, *«Deus»*, *«Omnipotens aeterne Deus»*, *«Pater»*, et cetera, aut variorum verborum supplicationem exprimentium, potest translationem efficere taediosam atque obscurare modum locuplem ac speciosum, quo in textu latino relatio inter fideles ac Deum significatur.

52. Translator nitatur servare «denotationem» seu sensum primarium verborum ac locutionum, quae in textu originali inveniuntur, necnon «connotationem» seu parva discrimina significationis vel affectus ab illis evocatam, et sic efficere, ut textus pateat aliis ordinibus significationis, qui fortasse consulto in textu originali erant quaesiti.

53. Quotiescumque vocabulum aliquod latinum significationem habet gravem, quam difficile est in linguam aetate nostra vigentem reddere (veluti verba *«munus»*, *«famulus»*, *«consubstantialis»*, *«propitius»*, etc.), in translatione adhiberi possunt variae rationes, sive eo quod vocabulum uno verbo sive pluribus coniunctis redditur sive ut vocabulum novum condatur, fortasse aptatum aut transcriptum diverso scribendi modo, respectu habito textus primigenii (cf. supra n. 21), sive inducendo vocabulum, quod iam habetur pluribus sensibus praeditum.[37]

---

37 Cf. Congr. de Cult. Div. et Disc. Sacr., Instr. *Varietates legitimae*, n. 53: AAS 87 (1995) 308.

vegetari, and *pasci*, on the one hand, or the nouns *caritas* and *dilectio* on the other, or the words *anima, animus, cor, mens,* and *spiritus,* to give some examples. Similarly, a deficiency in translating the varying forms of addressing God, such as *Domine, Deus, Omnipotens aeterne Deus, Pater,* and so forth, as well as the various words expressing supplication, may render the translation monotonous and obscure the rich and beautiful way in which the relationship between the faithful and God is expressed in the Latin text.

52. The translator should strive to maintain the denotation, or primary sense of the words and expressions found in the original text, as well as their connotation, that is, the finer shades of meaning or emotion evoked by them, and thus to ensure that the text be open to other orders of meaning that may have been intended in the original text.

53. Whenever a particular Latin term has a rich meaning that is difficult to render into a modern language (such as the words *munus, famulus, consubstantialis, propitius,* etc.) various solutions may be employed in the translations, whether the term be translated by a single vernacular word or by several, or by the coining of a new word, or perhaps by the adaptation, transcription, or transliteration of the same term into a language that is different from that of the original text (cf. above, n. 21), or the use of an already existing word which may bear various meanings.[37]

---

37 Cf. Congr. for Divine Worship and the Discipline of the Sacraments, Instr. *Varietates legitimae,* n. 53: AAS 87 (1995) 308.

54. In translationibus proclivitas ad rem psychologicam introducendam vitetur, quod fit praesertim cum loco locutionum, quae de virtutibus theologicis agunt, aliae ponuntur, quae mere ad motus affectionum humanarum referuntur. Quoad verba aut locutiones, quibus theologica notio causalitatis proprie divinae redditur (ex. gr., latine expressa verbis *«praesta, ut . . . »*), vitandum est, ipsorum loco, verba aut locutiones mere exteriorem aut profanam rationem auxilii ferendi significantia adhibere.

55. Nonnulla vocabula, quae in textum latinum liturgicum prima facie inducta esse videntur metri causa aut aliarum rationum pertinentium ad technicam disciplinam litterarum, revera saepe significationem proprie theologicam praebent, quapropter in translationibus, quantum fieri potest, servanda sunt. Necesse est, ut vocabula, quae aspectus mysteriorum fidei et christianorum animi rectum habitum exprimunt, accuratissime transferantur.

56. Vocabula quaedam, quae ad thesaurum pertinent totius Ecclesiae primaevae aut ad magnam eius partem, atque alia, quae ad humani ingenii patrimonium sunt adiuncta, in translatione observentur, quantum fieri potest, ad litteram, sicut verba responsionis populi *«Et cum spiritu tuo»* aut locutionis *«mea culpa, mea culpa, mea maxima culpa»* in actu paenitentiali Ordinis Missae.

54. To be avoided in translations is any psychologizing tendency, especially a tendency to replace words treating of the theological virtues by others expressing merely human emotions. As regards words or expressions conveying a properly divine notion of causality (e.g., those expressed in Latin by the words "*praesta, ut . . .*"), one should avoid employing words or expressions denoting a merely extrinsic or profane sort of assistance instead.

55. Certain words that may appear to have been introduced into the Latin liturgical text for reasons of meter or other technical or literary reasons convey, in reality, a properly theological content, so that they are to be preserved, insofar as possible, in the translation. It is necessary to translate with the utmost precision those words that express aspects of the mysteries of faith and the proper disposition of the Christian soul.

56. Certain expressions that belong to the heritage of the whole or of a great part of the ancient Church, as well as others that have become part of the general human patrimony, are to be respected by a translation that is as literal as possible, as for example the words of the people's response *Et cum spiritu tuo*, or the expression *mea culpa, mea culpa, mea maxima culpa* in the Act of Penance of the Order of Mass.

B. *De syntaxi, stylo ac genere litterario*

57. Indoles insignis Ritus romani, qui res enucleate breviter et pressius exprimit, in translatione, quantum fieri potest, servetur. Insuper in variis partibus librorum liturgicorum, quam opportunum videtur, eandem rationem pro eadem locutione transferenda servare. Haec principia sunt observanda:

a. Connexio inter enunciata, ut exstat, ex. gr. in locutionibus subordinatis et relativis, in verborum dispositione et variis rationibus parallelismi, plene, ut fieri potest, servetur modo linguae vulgari accommodato.

b. In translatione vocabulorum, quae in textu originali continentur, servetur, ut fieri potest, eadem persona, numerus, genus.

c. Significatio theologica verborum causalitatem, propositum aut eventum exprimentium (veluti *«ut»*, *«ideo»*, *«enim»* et *«quia»*), quamvis variae linguae diverso modo proferendi utantur, servetur.

d. Principia, supra ad n. 51 exposita, ad varietatem vocabulorum spectantia, observentur etiam quod attinet ad varietatem eorum syntaxis et styli (ex. gr., in positione intra Collectam vocabulorum, casu vocativo, ad Deum directorum).

B. Syntax, style and literary genre

57. That notable feature of the Roman Rite, namely its straightforward, concise and compact manner of expression, is to be maintained insofar as possible in the translation. Furthermore, the same manner of rendering a given expression is to be maintained throughout the translation of liturgical books, insofar as feasible. These principles are to be observed:

a. The connection between various expressions, as can be found, for example, in subordinate and relative clauses, the ordering of words, and various forms of parallelism, is to be maintained as completely as possible in a manner appropriate to the vernacular language.

b. In the translation of terms contained in the original text, the same person, number, and gender is to be maintained insofar as possible.

c. The theological significance of words expressing causality, purpose or consequence (such as *ut, ideo, enim,* and *quia*) is to be maintained, though different languages may employ varying means for doing so.

d. The principles set forth above, in n. 51, regarding variety of vocabulary, are to be observed also in the variety of syntax and style (for example, in the location within the Collect of the vocative addressed to God).

58. Genus litterarium et rhetoricum variorum textuum Liturgiae romanae servetur.[38]

59. Quoniam textibus liturgicis, ipsa eorum indole, propositum est ut ore proferantur et audiantur in celebratione liturgica, modi quidam dicendi eorum sunt propria, qui a communi loquendi consuetudine aut a textibus, qui tacite leguntur, differunt, velut exempla recurrentia et cognoscibilia syntaxis et styli, tonus sollemnis aut sublimis, agnominatio et consonantia, imagines concretae ac vividae, iteratio, parallelismus et discrepantiae, rhythmus quidam, et interdum vis lyrica operum poeticorum. Si fieri non potest, ut eadem elementa styli de textu primigenio in lingua vulgari usurpentur (ut saepe contingit, veluti cum de agnominatione vel de consonantia agitur), nihilominus translator oportet animadvertat horum elementorum quaesitum effectum in animum auditoris, quoad argumentum vel discrepantiam inter notiones vel emphasin, et cetera. Deinde cum aliqua sollertia uti debet omnibus facultatibus linguae vulgaris, ut integre, quantum fieri possit, eundem effectum assequatur, non solum quidem circa ipsum argumentum, sed etiam circa res alias. In textibus poeticis maior flexibilitas exquiratur in translatione, eo consilio, ut comprobari possit officium ipsius formae litterariae in argumento textus reddendo. Nihilominus

---

38 Cf. *ibidem*; cf. MISSALE ROMANUM, editio typica tertia: *Institutio Generalis*, n. 392.

58. The literary and rhetorical genres of the various texts of the Roman Liturgy are to be maintained.[38]

59. Since liturgical texts by their very nature are intended to be proclaimed orally and to be heard in the liturgical celebration, they are characterized by a certain manner of expression that differs from that found in everyday speech or in texts intended be read silently. Examples of this include recurring and recognizable patterns of syntax and style, a solemn or exalted tone, alliteration and assonance, concrete and vivid images, repetition, parallelism and contrast, a certain rhythm, and at times, the lyric of poetic compositions. If it is sometimes not possible to employ in the translation the same stylistic elements as in the original text (as often happens, for example, in the case of alliteration or assonance), even so, the translator should seek to ascertain the intended effect of such elements in the mind of the hearer as regards thematic content, the expression of contrast between elements, emphasis, and so forth. Then the translator should employ the full possibilities of the vernacular language skillfully in order to achieve as integrally as possible the same effect as regards not only the conceptual content itself, but the other aspects as well. In poetic texts, greater flexibility will be needed in translation in order to provide for the role played by the literary form itself in expressing the content of the texts.

---

38 Cf. *ibid.*; cf. Missale Romanum, editio typica tertia: *Institutio Generalis*, n. 392.

locutiones peculiare momentum doctrinale et spirituale habentes aut illae, quae peculiariter sunt pernotae, ad litteram transferantur, ut fieri potest.

60. Magna pars textuum liturgicorum ea est mente composita, ut canantur a sacerdote celebranti, a diacono, a cantore, a populo vel a schola cantorum. Quapropter textus transferatur oportet, ut idoneus fiat ad notas musicas. Attamen in textu notis musicis aptando plene attendatur ad auctoritatem textus ipsius, ita ut neque pro textibus e Sacra Scriptura neque pro iis e Liturgia desumptis, iam recognitione praeditis, paraphrases substituantur, eo spectantes, ut cantus facilior reddatur, neque hymni usurpentur, qui generatim aequales esse putentur.[39]

61. Textus cantui destinati peculiaris sunt momenti, cum fidelibus ingerant sensum sollemnitatis celebrationis atque unitatem in fide et caritate per unitatem vocum manifestent.[40] Hymni et cantica, quae in hodiernis editionibus typicis continentur, minimam partem constituunt immensi thesauri historici Ecclesiae Latinae atque valde expedit ut in editionibus lingua vulgari typis datis serventur, etiam una cum aliis, lingua vulgari immediate exaratis.

---

39   Cf. Missale Romanum, editio typica tertia: *Institutio Generalis*, nn. 53, 57.

40   Cf. Ioannes Paulus PP. II, Litt. Ap. *Dies Domini*, n. 50: AAS 90 (1998) 745.

Even so, expressions that have a particular doctrinal or spiritual importance or those that are more widely known are, insofar as possible, to be translated literally.

60. A great part of the liturgical texts are composed with the intention of their being sung by the priest celebrant, the deacon, the cantor, the people, or the choir. For this reason, the texts should be translated in a manner that is suitable for being set to music. Still, in preparing the musical accompaniment, full account must be taken of the authority of the text itself. Whether it be a question of the texts of Sacred Scripture or of those taken from the Liturgy and already duly confirmed, paraphrases are not to be substituted with the intention of making them more easily set to music, nor may hymns considered generically equivalent be employed in their place.[39]

61. Texts that are intended to be sung are particularly important because they convey to the faithful a sense of the solemnity of the celebration, and manifest unity in faith and charity by means of a union of voices.[40] The hymns and canticles contained in the modern *editiones typicae* constitute only the smallest part of the historic treasury of the Latin Church, and it is especially advantageous that they be preserved in the printed vernacular editions, even if placed there in addition to hymns composed originally in the vernacular language.

---

39 Cf. Missale Romanum, editio typica tertia: *Institutio Generalis*, nn. 53, 57.

40 Cf. Pope John Paul II, Apost. Letter *Dies Domini*, n. 50: AAS 90 (1998) 745.

Textus cum cantu edendi directo ipsa lingua vulgari compositi, potius depromantur de Sacra Scriptura atque de thesauro liturgico.

62. Textus quidam liturgici manu ecclesiastica compositi variis actionibus ritualibus sociantur peculiari habitu corporis, gestibus et usibus signorum expressis. Itaque in elaborandis aptis translationibus expedit, ut ad elementa attendatur sicut tempus ad textum recitandum necessarium, eius convenientiam cum recitatione vel cantu, aut cum continuis repetitionibus, etc.

4. Normae ad specialia textuum genera spectantes

A. *De Precibus eucharisticis*
63. Culmen totius actionis liturgicae est Missae celebratio, in qua, per vices, Prex Eucharistica seu Anaphora locum praecipuum obtinet.[41] Quapropter translationes Precum eucharisticarum approbatarum summa cum diligentia sunt parandae praesertim quoad formulas sacramentales, circa quas specialis procedendi ratio infra, ad nn. 85-86, praescribitur.

64. Revisiones translationum, quae postmodum sequantur, sine causis necessariis non debent notabiliter mutare textum vulgarem iam approbatum Precum Eucharisticarum, quas

---

41 MISSALE ROMANUM, editio typica tertia: *Institutio Generalis*, n. 78.

The texts for singing that are composed originally in the vernacular language would best be drawn from Sacred Scripture or from the liturgical patrimony.

62. Certain liturgical texts of ecclesiastical composition are associated with ritual actions expressed by a particular posture, gesture, or the use of signs. Thus, in preparing appropriate translations it will be advantageous to consider such factors as the time required for reciting the words, their suitability for being sung or recited, or for continuous repetition, etc.

4. Norms pertaining to special types of texts

A. *The Eucharistic Prayers*
63. The high point of all liturgical action is the celebration of the Mass, in which the Eucharistic Prayer or Anaphora in turn occupies a pre-eminent place.[41] For this reason, the approved translations of the approved Eucharistic Prayers require the utmost care, especially as regards the sacramental formulae, for which a particular procedure is prescribed below, in nn. 85-86.

64. Without real necessity, successive revisions of translations should not notably change the previously approved vernacular texts of the Eucharistic Prayers which the

---

41   Missale Romanum, editio typica tertia: *Institutio Generalis*, n. 78.

fideles gradatim memoria tenuerint. Quotiescumque translatio omnino nova necessario postulatur, observentur ea quae infra, ad n. 74, dicuntur.

B. *De Symbolo vel professione fidei*
65. Symbolum seu professio fidei eo tendit, ut universus populus congregatus verbo Dei in lectionibus e sacra Scriptura nuntiato et per homiliam exposito respondeat et ut regulam fidei proferendo formula pro usu liturgico probata magna fidei mysteria recolat et confiteatur.[42] Symbolum transferendum est verbis accuratis, quae traditio Ecclesiae Latinae ipsi tribuit, servato usu primae personae singularis, qua manifesto declaratur: «confessio fidei traditur in symbolo quasi ex persona totius Ecclesiae, quae per fidem unitur».[43] Insuper, verba «carnis resurrectionem» ad litteram sunt transferenda, quotiescumque Symbolum Apostolorum in Liturgia praescribitur vel adhiberi potest.[44]

C. *De «Praenotandis» ac textibus indolis rubricalis vel iuridicae*
66. Omnes partes uniuscuiusque libri liturgici eadem ratione transferri debent, qua in textu latino editionis typicae

---

42 Cf. *ibidem*, n. 67.

43 S. THOMAS AQUINAS, *Summa Theologiae*, IIa IIae, I, 9.

44 Cf. S. CONGR. PRO DOCTR. FIDEI, *Communicatio*, diei 2 decembris 1983: *Notitiae* 20 (1984) 181.

faithful will have committed gradually to memory. Whenever a completely new translation is necessary, the principles given below, in n. 74, are to be observed.

B. The Creed or Profession of Faith

65. By means of the Creed (*Symbolum*) or Profession of Faith, the whole gathered people of God respond to the word of God proclaimed in the Sacred Scriptures and expounded in the homily, recalling and confessing the great mysteries of the faith by means of a formula approved for liturgical use.[42] The Creed is to be translated according to the precise wording that the tradition of the Latin Church has bestowed upon it, including the use of the first person singular, by which is clearly made manifest that "the confession of faith is handed down in the Creed, as it were, as coming from the person of the whole Church, united by means of the Faith."[43] In addition, the expression *carnis resurrectionem* is to be translated literally wherever the Apostles' Creed is prescribed or may be used in the Liturgy.[44]

C. The "Praenotanda" and the texts of a rubrical or juridical nature

66. All parts of each liturgical book are to be translated in the same order in which they are set forth in the Latin text

---

42 Cf. *ibid.*, n. 67.

43 St. Thomas Aquinas, *Summa Theologiae*, IIa IIae, I, 9.

44 Cf. S. Congr. for the Doctrine of the Faith, *Communicatio*, 2 December 1983: *Notitiae* 20 (1984) 181.

ostenduntur, non exceptis institutione generali, praenotandis et instructionibus variis ritibus antepositis, necnon singulis rubricis, quae totius structurae Liturgiae sunt fulmentum.[45] Distinctio inter varia munera liturgica et appellationem ministrorum liturgicorum, propriis eorum titulis declaratis, ut in rubricis editionis typicae, in translatione accurate servetur, ratione, ut decet, habita eorum, quae supra, ad n. 50c, dicuntur.[46]

67. Ubi eiusmodi praenotanda aut alii textus editionum typicarum explicite postulant accommodationes aut definitiones, rem specifice indicantes, quae a Conferentiis inducantur, ex. gr., partes Missalis quae a Conferentia Episcoporum pressius definiendae sunt,[47] licet eiusmodi praescripta textui inserere, dummodo eiusmodi partes recognitionem Apostolicae Sedis acceperint. Ex natura rei, non expedit hoc in casu, ut eae partes transferantur adamussim, prout in editione typica exstant. Nihilominus, mentio fiat decretorum approbationis Conferentiae Episcoporum et recognitionis a Congregatione de Cultu Divino et Disciplina Sacramentorum concessae.

---

45 Cf. CONC. OECUM. VAT. II, Const. *Sacrosanctum Concilium*, n. 63b; S. CONGR. DE CULT. DIV., Declaratio «*De interpretationibus popularibus novorum textuum liturgicorum*», diei 15 septembris 1969: *Notitiae* 5 (1969) 333-334.

46 Cf. CONGR. PRO CLERICIS et al., Instr. *Ecclesiae de mysterio*, diei 15 augusti 1997, art. 1-3, 6-12: AAS 89 (1997) 861-865, 869-874.

47 Cf. MISSALE ROMANUM, editio typica tertia: *Institutio Generalis*, n. 389.

of the *editio typica*, including the *institutiones generales*, the *praenotanda*, and the instructions supplied in the various rites, which function as a support for the whole structure of the Liturgy.[45] The distinction between the various liturgical roles and the designation of the liturgical ministers by their proper titles is to be maintained in the translation precisely as it is in the rubrics of the *editio typica*, with due regard for the principles mentioned in n. 50c above.[46]

67. Wherever such *praenotanda* or other texts of the *editiones typicae* explicitly call for adaptations or specific applications to be introduced by the Conferences, as for example the parts of the Missal that are to be defined more specifically by the Conference of Bishops,[47] it is permissible to insert these prescriptions into the text, provided that they have received the *recognitio* of the Apostolic See. It is not required in such cases, by their very nature, to translate these parts verbatim as they stand in the *editio typica*. Nevertheless, a mention is to be made of the decree of approbation of the Conference of Bishops and of the *recognitio* granted by the Congregation for Divine Worship and the Discipline of the Sacraments.

---

45 Cf. Second Vatican Council, Const. *Sacrosanctum Concilium*, n. 63b; S. Congr. for Divine Worship, Decl. *De interpretationibus popularibus novorum textuum liturgicorum*, 15 September 1969: *Notitiae* 5 (1969) 333-334.

46 Cf. Congr. for the Clergy et al., Instr. *Ecclesiae de mysterio*, 15 August 1997, art. 1-3, 6-12: AAS 89 (1997) 861-865, 869-874.

47 Cf. Missale Romanum, editio typica tertia: *Institutio Generalis*, n. 389.

68. In popularium editionum initio collocentur decreta, quibus editiones typicae sunt promulgatae a Dicasterio competenti Apostolicae Sedis, ratione ducta praescriptionum ad n. 78 expositarum. Ponantur etiam decreta, per quae translationibus concessa est recognitio Sanctae Sedis, aut ipsa saltem recognitio concessa memoretur, additis die, mense, anno et numero protocolli decreti a Dicasterio emanati. Cum haec etiam monumenta historica sint, nomina Dicasteriorum aliorumve Apostolicae Sedis Institutorum accurate debent transferri, quod attinet ad diem promulgationis documenti, nec vero accommodari debent ad nunc vigens nomen eiusdem parisve institutionis.

69. Editiones librorum liturgicorum lingua vulgari apparatae omni ex parte congruant cum titulis, ordine textuum, rubricis et numerorum ratione, quae in editione typica exstant, nisi in praenotandis iisdem libris praepositis aliter statuatur. Inserantur insuper quaevis additamenta a Congregatione de Cultu Divino et Disciplina Sacramentorum approbata, sive in supplemento quodam seu appendice sive loco suo, prout Sedes Apostolica statuerit.

68. At the beginning of the vernacular editions are to be placed the decrees by which the *editiones typicae* have been promulgated by the competent Dicastery of the Apostolic See, with due regard for the prescriptions found in n. 78. Also to be placed there are the decrees by means of which the *recognitio* of the Holy See has been granted for the translations, or at least the mention of the *recognitio* is to be made together with the date, month, year, and protocol number of the decree issued by the Dicastery. Since these are also historical documents, the names of the Dicasteries or other organ of the Apostolic See are to be translated exactly as they appeared on the date of promulgation of the document, rather than being altered to reflect the present name of the same or equivalent body.

69. The editions of the liturgical books prepared in the vernacular language are to correspond in every part to the titles, the ordering of texts, the rubrics, and the system of numbering that appears in the *editio typica*, unless otherwise directed in the *praenotanda* of the same books. Furthermore, any additions approved by the Congregation for Divine Worship and the Discipline of the Sacraments are to be inserted either in a supplement or appendix, or in their proper place in the book, as the Apostolic See shall have directed.

III. De Translationum Praeparatione Deque Commissionum Erectione

1. De praeparandae alicuius translationis ratione

70. Propter officium Episcopis commissum translationes liturgicas procurandi,[48] id opus peculiariter committitur commissioni liturgicae, a Conferentia Episcoporum debite constitutae. Ubi talis commissio deest, munus translationem procurandi concredatur duobus vel tribus Episcopis, in studiis liturgicis, biblicis, philologicis aut musicis peritis.[49] Quod autem ad textuum perscrutationem et approbationem pertinet, omnes et singuli Episcopi hoc officium habere debent ut rem fiducialem directam, sollemnem et personalem.

71. In nationibus ubi plures linguae adhibentur, translationes in singulas linguas vulgares conficiantur et peculiari examini Episcoporum quorum interest subiciantur.[50] Nihilominus ad Conferentiam Episcoporum ut talem spectat ius et potestas circa omnes actus in hac Instructione memoratos ut ad huiusmodi Conferentiam pertinentes; ideoque ad totam Conferentiam spectat textum approbare et Apostolicae Sedi recognitionis causa subicere.

---

48 Cf. CONC. OECUM. VAT. II, Const. *Sacrosanctum Concilium*, n. 36; cf. *Codex Iuris Canonici*, can. 838 §3.

49 Cf. CONC. OECUM. VAT. II, Const. *Sacrosanctum Concilium*, n. 44; S. RITUUM CONGR., Instr. *Inter Oecumenici*, nn. 40b, 44; AAS 56 (1964) 885-886.

50 Cf. S. RITUUM CONGR., Instr. *Inter Oecumenici*, n. 40d; AAS 56 (1964) 886.

III. On the Preparation of Translations and the Establishment of Commissions

1. The manner of preparing a translation

70. Because the task of preparing liturgical translations is entrusted to the Bishops,[48] this work is committed in a particular way to the liturgical commission duly established by the Conference of Bishops. Wherever such a commission is lacking, the task of preparing the translation is to be entrusted to two or three Bishops who are expert in liturgical, biblical, philological or musical studies.[49] With respect to the examination and approbation of the texts, each and every Bishop must commit himself to this as a direct, solemn, and personal responsibility.

71. In nations where many languages are used, the translations into individual vernacular languages are to be prepared and submitted to the special examination of those Bishops involved.[50] Nevertheless, it is the Conference of Bishops as such that retains the right and the power to posit all of those actions mentioned in this Instruction as pertaining to the Conference; thus, it pertains to the full Conference to approve a text and to submit it for the *recognitio* of the Apostolic See.

---

48 Cf. Second Vatican Council, Const. *Sacrosanctum Concilium*, n. 36; cf. *Code of Canon Law*, can 838 § 3.

49 Cf. Second Vatican Council, Const. *Sacrosanctum Concilium*, n. 44; S. Congr. of Rites, Instr. *Inter Oecumenici*, nn. 40b, 44: AAS (1964) 885-886.

50 Cf. S. Congr. of Rites, Instr. *Inter Oecumenici*, n. 40d: AAS 56 (1964) 886.

72. Episcopi, in exsequendo munere eis commisso translationes textuum liturgicorum aptandi, diligenter provideant, ut translationes sint fructus nisus vere communis potius quam unius cuiusque personae aut coetus paucorum hominum.

73. Omnem promulgationem editionis typicae latinae alicuius libri liturgici subsequatur oportet tempestiva exaratio translationis eiusdem libri, quam Conferentia Episcoporum, post debitam eius approbationem, ad Congregationem de Cultu Divino et Disciplina Sacramentorum mittat, cuius est eam recognoscere secundum normas in hac Instructione expositas, aliisque iure servandis.[51] Si autem de mutatione alicuius tantummodo partis editionis typicae latinae vel de insertione quorundam elementorum novorum agitur, haec innovationes in omnibus editionibus, lingua populari effectis, quae sequentur, plene et fideliter serventur.

74. Stabilitas quaedam observetur oportet, quantum fieri potest, in editionibus, quae sequentur, lingua aliqua huius aetatis vigente confectis. Partes populi memoriae mandandae, praesertim si cum cantu eduntur, solum ob causam iustam atque magnam immutentur. Nihilominus, si mutationes maioris momenti necessariae fuerint eo consilio, ut textus aliquis ad normas, quae hac Instructione continentur, conformetur, melius erit ut omnes simul

---

51 Cf. *Codex Iuris Canonici*, can. 838.

72. The Bishops, in fulfilling their mission of preparing translations of liturgical texts, are carefully to ensure that the translations be the fruit of a truly common effort rather than of any single person or of a small group of persons.

73. Whenever a Latin *editio typica* of a given liturgical book is promulgated, it is necessary that it be followed in a timely manner by the preparation of a translation of the same book, which the Conference of Bishops is to send, after having duly approved it, to the Congregation for Divine Worship and the Discipline of the Sacraments, to which it pertains to grant the *recognitio* according to the norms set forth in this Instruction, and also in keeping with others established by the law.[51] However, when it is a question of a change affecting only a part of the Latin *editio typica* or the insertion of new elements, these new elements are to be maintained fully and faithfully in all succeeding editions produced in the vernacular language.

74. A certain stability ought to be maintained whenever possible in successive editions prepared in modern languages. The parts that are to be committed to memory by the people, especially if they are sung, are to be changed only for a just and considerable reason. Nevertheless, if more significant changes are necessary for the purpose of bringing the text into conformity with the norms contained in this Instruction, it will be preferable to make such changes at one

---

51 Cf. *Code of Canon Law*, can. 838.

producantur. Quod si fieri contingat, ad editionem novi textus accedat conveniens tempus catechesis.

75. Translatio librorum liturgicorum expostulat non solum rarum gradum peritiae, sed etiam spiritum orationis et fiduciam auxilii divini, quod non tantum translatoribus conceditur, sed ipsi Ecclesiae, per totum cursum ad approbationem textuum certam ac definitam perducendum. Animus paratus pati ut proprium opus ab aliis expendatur et revideatur, est pernecessarius habitus, quo quivis oportet sit insignis, qui munus liturgicos libros transferendi suscepit. Praeterea omnes translationes vel textus lingua vulgari exarati, non exceptis iis, quae ad praenotanda spectant, atque textus ad rubricas pertinentes oportet sint sine nomine auctoris, quod attinet sive ad personas sive ad instituta e pluribus constantia, ut fieri contingit in editionibus typicis.[52]

76. Ad statuta Concilii Vaticani II de sacra Liturgia in effectum ducenda, patet e maturatione experientiae quasi quattuor decenniorum instaurationis liturgicae a Concilio Oecumenico decursorum, necessitatem habere translationum textuum liturgicorum—saltem quoad linguas diffusiores—non solum Episcopos in Ecclesiis particularibus regendis, sed etiam ipsam Sedem Apostolicam, ut universalem erga christifideles sollecitudinem in Alma Urbe atque per orbem terrarum efficaciter agat. In dioecesi enim romana,

---

52   Cf. S. Congr. pro Cult. Div., Declaratio, diei 15 maii 1970: *Notitiae* 6 (1970) 153.

time, rather than prolonging them over the course of several editions. In such case, a suitable period of catechesis should accompany the publication of the new text.

75. The translation of liturgical texts requires not only a rare degree of expertise, but also a spirit of prayer and of trust in the divine assistance granted not only to the translators, but to the Church herself, throughout the whole process leading to the definitive approbation of the texts. The readiness to see one's own work examined and revised by others is an essential trait that should be evident in one who undertakes the translation of liturgical texts. Furthermore, all translations or texts prepared in vernacular languages, including those of the *praenotanda* and the rubrics, are to be anonymous with respect to persons as well as to institutions consisting of several persons, as in the case of the *editiones typicae*.[52]

76. In implementing the decisions of the Second Vatican Council, it has become evident from the mature experience of the nearly four decades of the liturgical renewal that have elapsed since the Council that the need for translations of liturgical texts—at least as regards the major languages—is experienced not only by the Bishops in governing the particular Churches, but also by the Apostolic See, for the effective exercise of her universal solicitude for the Christian faithful in the City of Rome and throughout the world. Indeed, in the Diocese of Rome, especially in many of the Churches and

---

52   Cf. S. Congr. for Divine Worship, Decl., 15 May 1970: *Notitiae* 6 (1970) 153.

praesertim in multis ecclesiis et institutis Urbis, quae
ab eadem dioecesi vel ab organis Sanctae Sedis aliquo
modo dependent, necnon in actuositate Dicasteriorum
Curiae Romanae et Repraesentantium Pontificiorum,
maiores linguae latius et frequentius adhibentur, etiam in
celebrationibus liturgicis. Quare visum est, ut in posterum,
quoad praedictas linguas maiores, Congregatio de Cultu
Divino et Disciplina Sacramentorum in translationibus
apparandis pressius seu intimius partem habeat.

77. Quod insuper ad linguas praecipuas attinet, integra
translatio omnium librorum liturgicorum tempore congruo
conficiatur. Translationes antehac ad interim approbatae
perficiantur aut omni ex parte revideantur, ut casus fert, ac
postea Episcopis subiciantur ad approbationem definitivam
secundum ea quae hac Instructione exponuntur, ac denique
ad Congregationem de Cultu Divino et Disciplina
Sacramentorum mittantur, ad Apostolicae Sedis
recognitionem impetrandam.[53]

78. Cum agitur de sermonibus minus diffusis, qui ad usum
liturgicum approbati sunt, transferri possunt in primis
maiores tantum ex libris liturgicis, secundum necessitates
pastorales, consentiente Congregatione de Cultu Divino et
Disciplina Sacramentorum. Singuli libri, qui sic seliguntur,
integre transferendi sunt, ut supra, ad n. 66, dicitur. Quod

---

53   Cf. IOANNES PAULUS PP. II, Litt. Ap. *Vicesimus quintus annus*, n. 20: AAS 81 (1989) 916.

institutes of the City that depend in some way on the Diocese or the organs of the Holy See, as well as in the activity of the Dicasteries of the Roman Curia and the Pontifical Representations, the major languages are widely and frequently employed even in liturgical celebrations. For this reason, it has been determined that in the future, the Congregation for Divine Worship and the Discipline of the Sacraments will be involved more immediately and directly in the preparation of the translations into these major languages.

77. Furthermore, as regards the major languages, an integral translation of all of the liturgical books is to be prepared in a timely manner. Translations heretofore approved *ad interim* are to be perfected or thoroughly revised, as the case requires, and afterwards submitted to the Bishops for definitive approbation in accordance with the norms set forth in this Instruction. Finally, they are to be sent to the Congregation for Divine Worship and the Discipline of the Sacraments with a request for the *recognitio*.[53]

78. In the case of the less diffused languages that are approved for liturgical use, the larger or more important liturgical books, in particular, may be translated, according to pastoral necessity and with the consent of the Congregation for Divine Worship and the Discipline of the Sacraments. The individual books thus selected are to be translated integrally, in the manner described in n. 66 above. As for the

---

53   Cf. Pope John Paul II, Apost. Letter *Vicesimus quintus annus*, n. 20: AAS 81 (1989) 916.

attinet ad decreta, institutionem generalem, praenotanda et instructiones, licet ea typis imprimi lingua, quae differt a lingua in celebratione adhibita et nihilominus prorsus intellegitur a sacerdotibus vel diaconis celebrantibus eo in territorio. Licet textum latinum decretorum typis imprimi aut translationi additum aut eius loco positum.

2. De approbatione translationis ac petitione recognitionis a Sede Apostolica impetrandae

79. Approbatio textuum liturgicorum, sive definitiva sive ad interim seu ad experimentum, fieri debet per decretum. Ut hoc legitime patretur, haec, quae sequuntur, oportet observentur.[54]

a. Ad legitima ferenda decreta, duae ex tribus suffragiorum secretorum partes requiruntur, ab omnibus iis qui in Conferentia Episcoporum iure fruuntur suffragium deliberativum ferendi.

b. Omnia acta ab Apostolica Sede probanda, in duplici exemplari exarata, a Praeside et Secretario Conferentiae subscripta sigilloque debite munita, ad Congregationem

---

54 Cf. CONC. OECUM. VAT. II, Const. *Sacrosanctum Concilium*, n. 36; PAULUS PP. VI, Litt. Ap. *Sacram Liturgiam*, IX: AAS 56 (1964) 143; S. RITUUM CONGR., Instr. *Inter Oecumenici*, nn. 27-29: AAS 56 (1964) 883; COMM. CENTRALIS COORDINANDIS POST CONCILIUM LABORIBUS ET CONCILII DECRETIS INTERPRETANDIS, Responsum ad propositum dubium: AAS 60 (1968) 361; cf. S. CONGR. PRO SACR. ET CULT. DIV., Ep. ad Praesides Conf. Episc. «*De linguis vulgaribus in S. Liturgiam inducendis*», diei 5 iunii 1976: *Notitiae* 12 (1976) 300-302.

decrees, the *institutio generalis*, the *praenotanda* and the instructions, it is permissible to print them in a language that is different from the one used in the celebration, but nevertheless intelligible to the priest or deacon celebrants in the same territory. It is permissible to print the Latin text of the decrees, either in addition to the translation or instead of it.

2. The approbation of the translation and the petition for the *recognitio* of the Apostolic See

79. The approbation liturgical texts, whether definitive, on the one hand, or *ad interim* or *ad experimentum* on the other, must be made by decree. In order that this be legitimately executed, the following are to be observed:[54]

a.   For the legitimate passage of decrees, a two-thirds vote by secret ballot is required on the part of all who enjoy the right to a deliberative vote of the Conference of Bishops.

b.   All acts to be examined by the Apostolic See, prepared in duplicate, signed by the President and Secretary of the Conference, and duly affixed with its seal, are to be

---

54   Cf. Second Vatican Council, Const. *Sacrosanctum Concilium*, n. 36; Pope Paul VI, Apost. Letter *Sacram Liturgiam*, IX: AAS 56 (1964) 143; S. Congr. of Rites, Instr. *Inter Oecumenici*, nn. 27-29: AAS 56 (1964) 883; Centr. Comm. for Coordinating Post-Conciliar Works and Interpreting the Decrees of the Council, Response to Dubium: AAS 60 (1968) 361; cf. S. Congr. for the Sacraments and Divine Worship, Letter to the Presidents of the Conferences of Bishops *De linguis vulgaribus in S. Liturgiam inducendis*, 5 June 1976: *Notitiae* 12 (1976) 300-302.

de Cultu Divino et Disciplina Sacramentorum sunt transmittenda. Illis actis contineantur:

   i.   nomina Episcoporum vel iure aequiparatorum, qui adunationi interfuerunt,

   ii.   relatio de rebus actis, qua contineri debet exitus suffragationum, ad singula decreta pertinentium, addito numero faventium, adversantium et se suffragii latione abstinentium.

c.   Duo exemplaria textuum liturgicorum vulgari sermone apparatorum mittantur; quantum fieri potest, idem textus praebeatur etiam per microdiscum instrumenti computatorii;

d.   In relatione peculiari, ea quae sequuntur, dilucide declarentur:[55]

   i.   rationes seu criteria in opere translationis servata,

   ii.   elenchus personarum in diversis laboris gradibus participantium, una cum brevi nota spectante ad ingenii qualitatem et peritiam uniuscuiusque earum,

---

55   Cf. S. Rituum Congr., Instr. *Inter Oecumenici*, n. 30: AAS 56 (1964) 883; S. Congr. pro Sacr. et Cult. Div., Ep. ad Praesides Conf. Episc. *«De linguis vulgaribus in S. Liturgiam inducendis»*, diei 5 iunii 1976: *Notitiae* 12 (1976) 302.

sent to the Congregation for Divine Worship and the Discipline of the Sacraments. In these acts are to be contained:

    i.   the names of the Bishops or of those equivalent in law who were present at the meeting,

    ii.   a *relatio* of the proceedings, which should contain the results of the voting for each individual decree, including the number in favor, the number opposed, and the number abstaining.

c.   Two copies are to be sent of the liturgical texts prepared in the vernacular language; insofar as possible, the same text should be sent on computer diskette;

d.   In the particular *relatio*, the following should be explained clearly:[55]

    i.   the process and criteria followed in the work of translation.

    ii.   a list of the persons participating at various stages in the work, together with a brief note describing the qualifications and expertise of each.

---

55 Cf. S. Congr. of Rites, Instr. *Inter Oecumenici*, n. 30: AAS 56 (1964) 883; S. Congr. For the Sacraments and Divine Worship, Letter to the Presidents of the Conferences of Bishops *De linguis vulgaribus in S. Liturgiam inducendis*, 5 June 1976: *Notitiae* 12 (1976) 302.

iii. mutationes fortasse inductae respectu prioris
translationis eiusdem editionis libri liturgici
distincte significentur una cum causis, cur
mutationes sint factae,

iv. expositio cuiusvis mutationis inductae circa
materiam editionis typicae latinae una cum
causis, ob quas id necessarium fuerit, et una
cum mentione prioris licentiae a Sede Apostolica
concessae ad huiusmodi mutationem inducendam.

80. Usus recognitionem a Sede Apostolica impetrandi pro
omnibus translationibus textuum liturgicorum[56] necessariam
praestat securitatem, significantem translationem esse
authenticam et cum textibus originalibus convenire, et
verum vinculum exprimit atque efficit communionis inter
beati Petri successorem et fratres in Episcopatu. Quae
insuper recognitio non est tantum formalitas quaedam, sed
actus potestatis regiminis, absolute necessarius (quo absente,
actus Conferentiae Episcoporum vi legis minime gaudet)
et quo imponi possunt modificationes, etiam substantiales.[57]
Quapropter nullos textus liturgicos translatos aut recenter
compositos typis imprimi licet quibus celebrantes aut
generatim populus utantur, si recognitio deest. Cum semper

---

56 Cf. CONC. OECUM. VAT. II, Const. *Sacrosanctum Concilium*, n. 36; S. RITUUM CONGR., Instr.
Inter Oecumenici, nn. 20-21, 31: AAS 56 (1964) 882, 884; *Codex Iuris Canonici*, can. 838.

57 Cf. PONT. COMM. CODICI IURIS RECOGNOSCENDO, Acta: *Communicationes* 15 (1983) 173.

iii. any changes that may have been introduced in relation to the previous translation of the same edition of the liturgical book are to be indicated clearly, together with the reasons for making such changes;

iv. an indication of any changes with respect to the content of the Latin *editio typica* together with the reasons which they were necessary, and with a notation of the prior consent of the Apostolic See for the introduction of such changes.

80. The practice of seeking the *recognitio* from the Apostolic See for all translations of liturgical books[56] accords the necessary assurance of the authenticity of the translation and its correspondence with the original texts. This practice both expresses and effects a bond of communion between the successor of blessed Peter and his brothers in the Episcopate. Furthermore, this *recognitio* is not a mere formality, but is rather an exercise of the power of governance, which is absolutely necessary (in the absence of which the act of the Conference of Bishops entirely in no way attains legal force); and modifications—even substantial ones—may be introduced by means of it.[57] For this reason it is not permissible to publish, for the use of celebrants or for the general public,

---

56 Cf. Second Vatican Council, Const. *Sacrosanctum Concilium*, n. 36; S. Congr. of Rites, Instr. *Inter Oecumenici*, nn. 20-21, 31: AAS (1964) 882, 884; *Code of Canon Law*, can. 838.

57 Cf. Pont. Comm. for the Revision of the Code of Canon Law, Acta: *Communicationes* 15 (1983) 173.

oporteat ut lex orandi cum lege credendi concordet ac
fidem christiani populi manifestet atque corroboret,
translationes liturgicae Deo dignae esse non poterunt
nisi ubertatem doctrinae catholicae de textu originali in
versionem vulgarem fideliter transferant, ita ut sermo
sacer accommodetur ad rem dogmaticam, quam continet.[58]
Observandum insuper est principium, iuxta quod
unaquaeque Ecclesia particularis cum Ecclesia universali
concordare debet non solum quoad fidei doctrinam et
signa sacramentalia, sed etiam quoad usus universaliter
acceptos ab apostolica et continua traditione;[59] ideoque
Apostolicae Sedis debita recognitio spectat ad invigilandum,
ut translationes ipsae, necnon legitimae quaedam varietates
in eas inductae, nedum populi Dei unitati noceant, ei potius
semper inserviant.[60]

81. Recognitio ab Apostolica Sede concessa in editione typis
excussa indicari debet una cum sententia *«concordat cum*

---

58 Cf. PAULUS PP. VI, Allocutio ad Sodales et Peritos Consilii «ad exsequendam
Constitutionem de S. Liturgia», diei 13 octobris 1966: AAS 58 (1966) 1146; Allocutio
ad Sodales et Peritos Consilii «ad exsequendam Constitutionem de S. Liturgia», diei
14 octobris 1968: AAS 60 (1968) 734.

59 MISSALE ROMANUM, editio typica tertia, *Institutio Generalis*, n. 397.

60 Cf. CONC. OECUM. VAT. II, Const. dogm. de Ecclesia *Lumen Gentium*, n. 13; cf. IOANNES
PAULUS PP. II, Litt. Ap. motu proprio datae, *Apostolos suos*, diei 21 maii 1998, n. 22: AAS
90 (1998) 655-656.

any liturgical texts that have been translated or recently composed, as long as the *recognitio* is lacking. Since the *lex orandi* must always be in harmony with the *lex credendi* and must manifest and support the faith of the Christian people, the liturgical translations will not be capable of being worthy of God without faithfully transmitting the wealth of Catholic doctrine from the original text into the vernacular version, in such a way that the sacred language is adapted to the dogmatic reality that it contains.[58] Furthermore, it is necessary to uphold the principle according to which each particular Church must be in accord with the universal Church not only as regards the doctrine of the Faith and the sacramental signs, but also as regards those practices universally received through Apostolic and continuous tradition.[59] For these reasons, the required *recognitio* of the Apostolic See is intended to ensure that the translations themselves, as well as any variations introduced into them, will not harm the unity of God's people, but will serve it instead.[60]

81. The *recognitio* granted by the Apostolic See is to be indicated in the printed editions together with the *concordat cum*

---

58   Cf. Pope Paul VI, Address to the Members and Experts of the Consilium "for the implementation of the Constitution on the Sacred Liturgy," 13 October 1966: AAS 58 (1966) 1146; Address to the Members and Experts of the Consilium "for the implementation of the Constitution on the Sacred Liturgy" 14 October 1968: AAS 60 (1968) 734.

59   Missale Romanum, editio typica tertia, *Institutio Generalis*, n. 397.

60   Cf. Second Vatican Council, Dogm. Const. On the Church, *Lumen Gentium*, n. 13; cf. Pope John Paul II, Apost. Letter (Motu proprio) *Apostolos suos*, 21 May 1998, n. 22: AAS 90 (1998) 655-656.

originali», cui Praeses Commissionis liturgicae Conferentiae Episcoporum subscripserit nec sine vocabulo «*imprimatur*», a Praeside eiusdem Conferentiae subnotato.[61] Praeterea duo exemplaria cuiusvis editionis typis impressae mittantur ad Congregationem de Cultu Divino et Disciplina Sacramentorum.[62]

82. Quaevis mutatio in libro liturgico, a Conferentia Episcoporum iam approbato cum subsecuta recognitione Apostolicae Sedis, spectans ad selectionem textuum ex libris liturgicis iam editis vel mutationem dispositionis textuum, fieri debet secundum modum procedendo, supra n. 79 statutum, ratione etiam habita praescriptionum supra, ad n. 22, expositarum. Quaelibet alia ratio procedendi in peculiaribus rerum adiunctis adhiberi potest solummodo, si per Statuta Conferentiae Episcoporum aut per aequalem legislationem, a sede Apostolica approbatum, ea sit sancita.[63]

83. Ad editiones librorum liturgicorum lingua vulgari exaratas quod attinet, intellegendum est Conferentiae Episcoporum approbationem, necnon Apostolicae Sedis recognitionem, solummodo pro territorio eiusdem

---

61 Cf. *Codex Iuris Canonici*, can. 838 §3.

62 Cf. S. Congr. de Sacr. et Cult. Div., Ep. ad Praesides Conf. Episc. «*De linguis vulgaribus in S. Liturgiam inducendis*», diei 5 iunii 1976: *Notitiae* 12 (1976) 302.

63 Cf. *ibidem*, pp. 300-302.

originali signed by the chairman of the liturgical commission of the Conference of Bishops, as well as the *imprimatur* undersigned by the President of the same Conference.[61] Afterwards, two copies of each printed edition are to be sent to the Congregation for Divine Worship and the Discipline of the Sacraments.[62]

82. Any alteration of a liturgical book that has already been approved by the Conference of Bishops with the subsequent *recognitio* of the Apostolic See, as regards either the selection of texts from liturgical books already published or the changing of the arrangement of the texts, must be done according to the procedure established above, in n. 79, with due regard also for the prescriptions set forth in n. 22. Any other manner of proceeding in particular circumstances may be employed only if it is authorized by the Statutes of the Conference of Bishops or equivalent legislation approved by the Apostolic See.[63]

83. As regards the editions of liturgical books prepared in vernacular languages, the approbation of the Conference of Bishops as well as the *recognitio* of the Apostolic See are to be regarded as valid only for the territory of the same

---

61 Cf. *Code of Canon Law*, can. 838 § 3.

62 Cf. S. Congr. for the Sacraments and Divine Worship, Letter to the Presidents of the Conferences of Bishops *De linguis vulgaribus in S. Liturgiam inducendis*, 5 June 1976: *Notitiae* 12 (1976) 302.

63 Cf. *ibid.*, 300-302.

Conferentiae valere, neque has editiones sine Apostolicae
Sedis licentia in alio territorio adhiberi posse, exceptis in
peculiaribus rerum adiunctis, prout supra, ad nn. 18 et 76,
memorata sunt, servatisque normis ibi expositis.

84. Ubi Conferentia quaedam Episcoporum bonis vel
instrumentis sufficientibus ad librum liturgicum apparandum
atque imprimendum careat, Praeses ipsius Conferentiae
rem exponat Congregationi de Cultu Divino et Disciplina
Sacramentorum, cuius est quamvis aliam dispositionem
aut capere aut approbare, quoad libros liturgicos una
cum aliis Conferentiis editos illosve alibi iam adhibitos
usurpandos. Quae vero licentia Sanctae Sedis solummodo
ad actum conceditur.

3. De translatione et approbatione formularum sacramentalium

85. Circa translationes formularum sacramentalium, quas
Congregatio de Cultu Divino iudicio Summi Pontificis
subicere debet, sequentia sunt observanda, praeter ea quae
ad translationem aliorum textuum liturgicorum requiruntur:[64]

---

64 Cf. S. CONGR. PRO CULT. DIV., Ep. ad Praesides Conf. Episc. «De normis servandis quoad
    libros liturgicos in vulgus edendos, illorum translatione in linguas hodiernas peracta», diei 25
    octobris 1973: AAS 66 (1974) 98-99; S. CONGR. DE SACR. ET CULT. DIV., Ep. ad Praesides
    Conf. Episc. «De linguis vulgaribus in S. Liturgiam inducendis», diei 5 iunii 1976: Notitiae 12
    (1976) 300-302.

Conference, so that these editions may not be used in another territory without the consent of the Apostolic See, except in those particular circumstances mentioned above, in nn. 18 and 76, and in keeping with the norms set forth there.

84. Wherever a certain Conference of Bishops lacks sufficient resources or instruments for the preparation and printing of a liturgical book, the President of the that Conference is to explain the situation to the Congregation for Divine Worship and the Discipline of the Sacraments, to which it pertains to establish or to approve any different arrangement, such as the publication of liturgical books together with other Conferences or the use of those already employed elsewhere. Such a concession shall only be granted by the Holy See *ad actum*.

3. On the translation and approbation of sacramental formulae

85. As regards the translation of the sacramental formulae, which the Congregation for Divine Worship must submit to the judgment of the Supreme Pontiff, the following principles are to be observed besides those required for the translation of other liturgical texts:[64]

---

64 Cf., S. Congr. For Divine Worship, Letter to the Presidents of the Conferences of Bishops *De normis servandis quoad libros liturgicos in vulgus edendos, illorum translatione in linguas hodiernas peracta*, 25 October 1973: AAS 66 (1974) 98-99; S. Congr. for the Sacraments and Divine Worship, Letter to the Presidents of the Conferences of Bishops *De linguis vulgaribus in S. Liturgiam inducendis*, 5 June 1976: *Notitiae* 12 (1976) 300-302.

a. Cum de linguis anglica, gallica, germanica, hispanica, italica, lusitana agitur, omnia acta, singulis linguis conscripta, praesententur;

b. Si translatio a textu vulgari iam eadem lingua composito et approbato discrepat, oportet exponatur causa, ob quam mutatio est inducta;

c. Praeses et Secretarius Conferentiae Episcoporum testari debent translationem a Conferentia Episcoporum esse approbatam.

86. Cum de linguis minus diffusis agitur, omnia peragantur, ut supra sunt exposita. Acta tamen una ex linguis supra dictis, quae latius sunt cognitae, redigeri debent summa cura, ita ut significatio uniuscuiusque verbi linguae vulgaris reddatur. Praeses et Secretarius Conferentiae Episcoporum, postquam peritos, ut necesse est, fiducia dignos consuluerunt, authenticitatem huius translationis testificentur.[65]

4. De unica versione textuum liturgicorum
87. Commendatur ut habeatur unica pro unoquoque vulgari sermone versio librorum aliorumque textuum liturgicorum,

---

65 Cf. S. Congr. pro Cult. Div., Ep. ad Praesides Conf. Episc. «*De normis servandis quoad libros liturgicos in vulgus edendos, illorum translatione in linguas hodiernas peracta*», diei 25 octobris 1973: AAS 66 (1974) 98-99; S. Congr. de Sacr. et Cult. Div., Ep. ad Praesides Conf. Episc. «*De linguis vulgaribus in S. Liturgiam inducendis*», diei 5 iunii 1976: *Notitiae* 12 (1976) 300-302.

a.   In the case of the English, French, German, Italian, Portuguese and Spanish languages, all of the acts are to be presented in that language;

b.   If the translation differs from a vernacular text already prepared and approved in the same language, it is necessary to explain the reason for the introduction of the change;

c.   The President and Secretary of the Conference of Bishops should testify that the translation has been approved by the Conference of Bishops.

86. In the case of the less widely diffused languages, everything shall be prepared as set forth above. The acts, however, are to be prepared with great care in one of the languages mentioned above as more widely known, rendering the meaning of each individual word of the vernacular language. The President and Secretary of the Conference of Bishops, after any necessary consultation with trustworthy experts, are to testify to the authenticity of the translation.[65]

4. On a unified version of the liturgical texts

87. It is recommended that there be a single translation of the liturgical books for each vernacular language, brought

---

65   Cf. S. Congr. for Divine Worship, Letter to the Presidents of the Conferences of Bishops *De normis servandis quoad libros liturgicos in vulgus edendos, illorum translatione in linguas hodiernas peracta*, 25 October 1973: AAS 66 (1974) 98-99; S. Congr. for the Sacraments and Divine Worship, Letter to the Presidents of the Conferences of Bishops *De linguis vulgaribus in S. Liturgiam inducendis*, 5 June 1976: *Notitiae* 12 (1976) 300-302.

consilio inito inter Episcopos regionum ubi eadem lingua viget.[66] Si propter rerum adiuncta, id reapse fieri non potest, singulae Conferentiae Episcoporum, praevia consultatione Sanctae Sedis, statuant aut translationem, quae iam habetur, esse accommodandam aut novam apparandam. In utroque casu exquiratur actuum recognitio ex parte Congregationis de Cultu Divino et Disciplina Sacramentorum.

88. Si de Ordine Missae iisque partibus sacrae Liturgiae agitur, quae directam populi participationem requirunt, unica habeatur translatio certa quadam lingua composita,[67] nisi aliter, singulis in casibus, provideatur.

89. Textus qui pluribus Conferentiis communes sunt, ut supra, ad nn. 87-88, ab omnibus et singulis Conferentiis Episcoporum, quae iis uti debent, de more approbandi sunt, antequam eorundem textuum confirmatio ab Apostolica Sede concedatur.[68]

90. Debito habito respectu traditionum catholicarum atque omnium principiorum et normarum, quae hac Instructione

---

66 Cf. S. Congr. pro Cult. Div., Normae «*De unica interpretatione textuum liturgicorum*», diei 6 februarii 1970: *Notitiae* 6 (1970) 84-85; cf. S. Rituum Congr., Instr. *Inter Oecumenici*, n. 40c: AAS 56 (1964) 886.

67 Cf. S. Congr. pro Cult. Div., Normae «*De unica interpretatione textuum liturgicorum*», diei 6 februarii 1970: *Notitiae* 6 (1970) 84-85.

68 Cf. *ibidem*, p. 85.

about by means of coordination among the Bishops of those regions where the same language is spoken.[66] If this proves truly impossible because of the circumstances, the individual Conferences of Bishops, after consultation with the Holy See, may decide either to adapt a previously existing translation or to prepare a new one. In either case, the *recognitio* of their acts is to be sought from the Congregation for Divine Worship and the Discipline of the Sacraments.

88. In regard to the Order of Mass and those parts of the Sacred Liturgy that call for the direct participation of the people, a single translation should exist in a given language,[67] unless a different provision is made in individual cases.

89. Texts which are common to several Conferences, as mentioned above in nn. 87-88, are ordinarily to be approved by each of the individual Conferences of Bishops which must use them, before the confirmation of the texts is granted by the Apostolic See.[68]

90. With due regard for Catholic traditions and for all of the principles and norms contained in this Instruction, an

---

66   Cf. S. Congr. For Divine Worship, Norms *De unica interpretatione textuum liturgicorum*, 6 February 1970: *Notitiae* 6 (1976) 84-85; cf. S. Congr. of Rites, Instr. *Inter Oecumenici*, n. 40c: AAS 56 (1964) 886.

67   Cf. S. Congr. for Divine Worship, Norms *De unica interpretatione textuum liturgicorum*, 6 February 1970: *Notitiae* 6 (1970) 84-85.

68   Cf. *ibid.*, 85.

continentur, aptus quidam nexus seu coordinatio maxime optatur, ubicumque fieri potest, inter quasvis translationes, communi usui destinatas in variis Ritibus Ecclesiae Catholicae, praesertim circa textus sacrae Scripturae. Episcopi Ecclesiae Latinae hanc rem foveant in spiritu obsequentis fraternaeque cooperationis.

91. Similis consensus exoptatur etiam cum Ecclesiis Orientalibus particularibus non Catholicis aut cum auctoritatibus ecclesialium communitatum Protestantium,[69] dummodo ne agatur de textu liturgico ad res doctrinales adhuc disputatas spectante, ac dummodo Ecclesiae vel communitates ecclesiales, de quibus agitur, sectatores habeant sat multos atque ii, qui consuluntur, vere vice fungantur earundem communitatum ecclesialium. Ut periculum scandali aut confusionis inter christifideles omnino vitetur, Ecclesia catholica plenam agendi libertatem in eiusmodi conventionibus, etiam in iure civili, debet servare.

5. De commissionibus «mixtis»

92. Apostolica Sedes, ut unitas librorum liturgicorum etiam in linguas populares translatorum haberetur neque bona et conatus Ecclesiae frustra consumerentur, promovit, inter

---

69 Cf. Conc. Oecum. Vat. II, Const. *Dei Verbum*, n. 22; *Codex Iuris Canonici*, can. 825 §2; Pont. Cons. ad Unitatem christianorum fovendam, *Directorium Oecumenicum*, diei 25 martii 1993, nn. 183-185, 187: AAS 85 (1993) 1104-1106; cf. *Codex Canonum Ecclesiarum Orientalium*, can. 655 §1.

appropriate relationship or coordination is greatly to be desired, whenever possible, between any translations intended for common use in the various Rites of the Catholic Church, especially as regards the text of Sacred Scripture. The Bishops of the Latin Church are to foster the same in a spirit of respectful and fraternal cooperation.

91. A similar agreement is desirable also with the particular non-Catholic Eastern Churches or with the authorities of the Protestant ecclesial communities,[69] provided that it is not a question of a liturgical text pertaining to doctrinal matters still in dispute, and provided also that the Churches or ecclesial communities involved have a sufficient number of adherents and that those consulted are truly capable of functioning as representatives of the same ecclesial communities. In order completely to avoid the danger of scandal or of confusion among the Christian faithful, the Catholic Church must retain full liberty of action in such agreements, even in civil law.

5. On "mixed" commissions

92. So that there might be unity in the liturgical books even as regards vernacular translations, and so that the resources and the efforts of the Church might not be consumed needlessly, the Apostolic See has promoted, among other possible

---

69 Cf. Second Vatican Council, Const. *Dei Verbum*, n. 22; *Code of Canon Law*, can. 825 § 2; Pont. Council for Promoting Christian Unity, *Directorium Oecumenicum*, 25 March 1993, nn. 183-185, 187: AAS 85 (1993) 1104-1106; cf. *Code of Canons of the Eastern Churches*, can. 655 § 1.

alias solutiones, quae fieri possint, erectionem commissionum «mixtarum», idest earum, quarum operis plures Conferentiae Episcoporum quodammodo participant.[70]

93. Congregatio de Cultu Divino et Disciplina Sacramentorum huiusmodi commissionem «mixtam», petentibus Conferentiis Episcoporum, ad quas res spectat, erigit; commissio deinceps secundum statuta ab Apostolica Sede approbata gubernatur.[71] Licet de more auspicandum sit ut de praedicta erectione poscenda necnon de redactione statutorum discernerentur omnes et singulae Conferentiae Episcoporum, quae commissionis quodammodo participant, priusquam de iisdem petitio Congregationi de Culto Divino et Disciplina Sacramentorum subiicitur, tamen, si ob magnum numerum earum Conferentiarum vel ob tempus protractior, quod ad suffragium peragendum forte requiritur, vel ob peculiarem necessitatem pastoralem visum erit praedicto Dicasterio, minime excluditur, ut statuta ab eodem, collatis consiliis, in quantum fieri poterit, aliquorum saltem Episcoporum quibus interest, et exarentur et approbentur.

---

70 Cf. CONSILIUM «AD EXSEQUENDAM CONSTITUTIONEM DE S. LITURGIA», *Ep. Praesidis*, diei 16 octobris 1964: *Notitiae* 1 (1965) 195; PAULUS PP. VI, Allocutio habita iis qui operam dant liturgicis textibus in vulgares linguas convertendis, diei 10 novembris 1965: AAS 57 (1965) 969; S. CONGR. DE CULT. DIV., *Normae de unica interpretatione textuum liturgicorum*, diei 6 februarii 1970: *Notitiae* 6 (1970) 84-85.

71 Cf. S. RITUUM CONGR., Instr. *Inter Oecumenici*, n. 23c: AAS 56 (1964) 882; *Codex Iuris Canonici*, cann. 94, 117, 120; cf. IOANNES PAULUS PP. II, Const. Ap. *Pastor Bonus*, diei 28 iunii 1988, art. 65: AAS 80 (1988) 877.

solutions, the establishment of "mixed" commissions, that is, those in whose work several Conferences of Bishops participate.[70]

93. The Congregation for Divine Worship and the Discipline of the Sacraments erects such "mixed" commissions at the request of the Conferences of Bishops involved; afterwards the commission is governed by statutes approved by the Apostolic See.[71] It is ordinarily to be hoped that each and every one of the Conferences of Bishops will have deliberated the matter of the above-mentioned establishment of the commission as well as of the composition of its statutes before the petition is submitted to the Congregation for Divine Worship and the Discipline of the Sacraments. Even so, if it is judged opportune by that Dicastery due to the great number of Conferences, or the protracted period of time required for a vote, or particular pastoral necessity, it is not excluded that the statutes be prepared and approved by the same Dicastery, after consultation, insofar as possible, with at least some of the Bishops involved.

---

70 Cf. Consilium "for the implementation of the Constitution on the Sacred Liturgy," Letter of the President, 16 October 1964: *Notitiae* 1 (1965) 195; Pope Paul VI, Address to translators of liturgical texts into vernacular languages, 10 November 1965: AAS 57 (1965) 969; S. Congr. for Divine Worship, Norms *De unica interpretatione textuum liturgicorum*, 6 February 1970: *Notitiae* 6 (1970) 84-85.

71 Cf. S. Congr. of Rites, Instr. *Inter Oecumenici*, n. 23c: AAS 56 (1964) 882; *Code of Canon Law*, cann. 94, 117, 120; Cf. Pope John Paul II, Apost. Const. *Pastor Bonus*, 28 June 1988, art. 65: AAS 80 (1988) 877.

94. Commissio «mixta», suo indole proprio, adiumentum praebet Episcopis neque pro iis substituitur, quod ad eorum munus pastorale aut cum Apostolica Sede relationes pertinet.[72] Commissio enim «mixta» tertium quid non constituit inter Sedem Apostolicam et Conferentias Episcoporum posita, nec aestimanda est via communicationis inter ipsas. Membra commissionis semper sunt Episcopi, vel saltem Episcopo iure aequiparati. Episcoporum insuper est, ut Membra eiusdem, Commissionem dirigere.

95. Expedit ut inter Episcopos, qui operis uniuscuiusque Commissionis «mixtae» sunt participes, aliqui saltem sint, quibus est creditum circa res liturgicas in suis cuiusque Conferentiis tractandas, utpote, ex. gr., Praesidibus commissionis Conferentiae de re liturgica.

96. Eiusmodi enim commissio, quantum fieri potest, ope commissionum liturgicarum a singulis Conferentiis Episcoporum dependentium, quae rei intersunt, sive quoad peritos sive quoad instrumenta technica adhibenda sive quoad auxilium «secretariale», officium suum exercet. Praesertim per coordinationem laboris incepti operatur, ita ex. gr. ut a commissione liturgica unius Conferentiae Episcoporum primum schema translationis praeparatur, ab aliis deinde commissionibus, etiam ob diversitatem locutionum eadem lingua in singulis territoriis sponte adhibitis, in melius mutatur.

---

72 Cf. IOANNES PAULUS PP. II, Litt. Ap. *Apostolos suos*, diei 21 maii 1998, nn. 18-19: AAS 90 (1998) 653-654.

94. A "mixed" commission, by its very nature, provides assistance to the Bishops rather than substituting for them as regards their pastoral mission and their relations with the Apostolic See.[72] For a "mixed" commission does not constitute a *tertium quid* place between the Conferences of Bishops and the Holy See, nor is it to be regarded as a means of communication between them. The Members of the Commission are always Bishops, or at least those equivalent in law to Bishops. It pertains to the Bishops, furthermore, to direct the Commission as its Members.

95. It would be advantageous that among the Bishops who participate in the work of each "mixed" commission, there be at least some who are responsible for dealing with liturgical matters in their respective Conferences, as, for example, the chairman of the liturgical commission of the Conference.

96. Such a commission, in fact, insofar as possible, should exercise its office by means of the resources of the liturgical commissions of the individual Conferences involved, using their experts, their technical resources, and their secretarial staff. For example, the work undertaken is coordinated in such a way that a first draft of the translation is prepared by the liturgical commission of one Conference and then improved by the other Conferences, even in light of the diversity of expression prevailing in the same language in the individual territories.

---

72 Cf. Pope John Paul II, Apost. Letter *Apostolos suos*, 21 May 1998, nn. 18-19: AAS 90 (1998) 653-654.

97. Expedit ut in singulis laboris temporibus, eiusdem operis aliqui saltem Episcopi participent, donec textus maturus Coetui Plenario Conferentiae Episcoporum examinandus et approbandus praesentetur et immediate a Conferentiae Preside, subscribente etiam Secretario Generali, ad normam iuris Sedi Apostolicae ad recognitionem mittatur.

98. Insuper Commissiones «mixtae» limites sibi ponant eo quod solum textus editionum typicarum pertractant, omittentes omnem rem theoreticam ad hoc earum opus non directe pertinentem, neque cum aliis Commissionibus «mixtis» relationes habeant neque novos textus componant.

99. Firma enim manet necessitas commissiones de sacra Liturgia necnon de musica sacra et arte sacra ad normam iuris in unaquaque dioecesi et territorio Conferentiae Episcoporum erigendi.[73] Hae omnes ad proprium finem obtinendum per se ipsas laborent, ne res ipsis commissas ad quandam commissionem «mixtam» tractanda transeant.

100. Ex qualibet Commissione «mixta» omnes praecipui cooperatores, qui non sint Episcopi quibusque munus ab his commissionibus stabiliter sit mandatum, antequam munus suum incipiant, declarationem indigent *«Nihil obstat»* a

---

73 Cf. Pius PP. XII, Litt. Enc. *Mediator Dei*, diei 20 novembris 1947: AAS 39 (1947) 561-562; Conc. Oecum. Vat. II, Const. *Sacrosanctum Concilium*, nn. 44-46; Paulus PP. VI, Litt. Ap. *Sacram Liturgiam*: AAS 56 (1964) 141; S. Rituum Congr., Instr. *Inter Oecumenici*, nn. 44-46: AAS 56 (1964) 886-887.

97. It is preferable that at least some Bishops participate at the various stages of work on a given text, until the time when the mature text is submitted to the Plenary Assembly of the Conference of Bishops for its examination and approval and is then sent immediately by the Conference President, with the signature also of the Secretary General, to the Apostolic See for the *recognitio*.

98. In addition, the "mixed" commissions are to limit themselves to the translation of the *editiones typicae*, leaving aside all theoretical questions not directly related to this work, and not involving themselves either in relations with other "mixed" commissions or in the composition of original texts.

99. In fact, the necessity remains for establishing commissions dealing with the Sacred Liturgy as well as sacred art and sacred music according to the norm of law in each diocese and territory of the Conference of Bishops.[73] These commissions shall work in their own right for the purposes proper to them, and shall not cede the matters entrusted to them to any "mixed" commission.

100. All of the principal collaborators of any "mixed" commission who are not Bishops, and to whom a stable mission is entrusted by such commissions, require the *nihil obstat*

---

73 Cf. Pope Pius XII, Encycl. Letter *Mediator Dei*, 20 November 1947: AAS 39 (1947) 561-562; Second Vatican Council, Const. *Sacrosanctum Concilium*, nn. 44-46; Pope Paul VI, Apost. Letter *Sacram Liturgiam*: AAS 56 (1964) 141; S. Congr. of Rites, Instr. *Inter Oecumenici*, nn. 44-46: AAS 56 (1964) 886-887.

Congregatione de Cultu Divino et Disciplina Sacramentorum concessam, perpensis titulis academicis ac testimoniis ad peritiam spectantibus, attentisque litteris commendatitiis proprii Episcopi dioecesani. In statutis conficiendis, ut supra ad n. 93 est dictum, accuratius describatur, quomodo haec petitio erit postulanda.

101. Omnes, non exceptis peritis, operam conferre debent sine nomine scripto et secreto observato qua condicione cuncti, praeter Episcopos, obligentur vi pactionis.

102. Expedit etiam, ut per temporis intervalla, Statutis definita, munera membrorum, cooperatorum et peritorum renoventur. Propter necessitates usu cognitas, quibus Commissiones quaedam premuntur, Congregatio de Cultu Divino et Disciplina Sacramentorum, poterit, si res ab ea postulatur, per indultum concedere, ut temporis spatium quibusdam membris, cooperatoribus aut peritis statutum, prorogetur.

103. Quod ad Commissiones «mixtas» iam exstantes attinet, statuta earum ad normam n. 93 ceterorumque hac ab Instructione praescriptorum revidenda sunt intra biennium, a die quo vigere incipit haec Instructio.

granted by the Congregation for Divine Worship and the Discipline of the Sacraments before beginning their work. The *nihil obstat* will be granted after consideration of their academic degrees and testimonies regarding their expertise, and a letter of recommendation submitted by their own diocesan Bishop. In the preparation of the statutes mentioned above, in n. 93, the manner in which the request for the *nihil obstat* is to be made shall be described with greater precision.

101. All, including the experts, are to conduct their work anonymously, observing confidentiality to which all who are not Bishops are to be bound by contract.

102. It is also advantageous that the terms of office of the members, collaborators and experts be renewed periodically in a manner defined by the Statutes. On account of a need on the part of the Commissions that may become evident in the course of the work, the Congregation for Divine Worship and the Discipline of the Sacraments may grant, upon request, a prolongation by indult of the term of office established for a particular member, collaborator or expert.

103. In the case of previously existing "mixed" Commissions, their statutes are to be revised within two years from the date that this Instruction enters into force, according to the norms of n. 93 and of the other norms prescribed by this Instruction.

104. Ob bonum fidelium, Sancta Sedes sibi reservat ius translationes in quamlibet linguam apparandi et ad usum liturgicum approbandi.[74] Attamen, etiamsi interdum in translationibus apparandis Sedes Apostolica per Congregationem de Cultu Divino et Disciplina Sacramentorum necessario interveniet, approbatio earundem, ut in usum liturgicum intra fines cuiusvis territorii ecclesiastici assumerentur, spectare pergat ad competentem Conferentiam Episcoporum, nisi aliud, in decreto approbationis eiusdem translationis a Sede Apostolica promulgato, diserte provideatur. Deinde Conferentia decretum approbationis pro illo territorio recognitionis causa remittat Sanctae Sedis, una cum textu ipso, ad normam huius Instructionis ceterorumque iuris statutorum.

105. Moventibus causis ut supra, ad nn. 76 et 84, expositis, aliisve necessitatibus pastoralibus urgentibus, commissiones, consilia, comitatus vel coetus laboris per decretum Congregationis de Cultu Divino et Disciplina Sacramentorum eriguntur, quae de translationibus sive singulorum quorundam librorum liturgicorum sive plurium, in una vel pluribus linguis, tractant, quaeque directo ex Apostolica Sede pendent. Quo

---

74 *Codex Iuris Canonici*, cann. 333, 360; IOANNES PAULUS PP. II, Const. Ap. *Pastor Bonus*, diei 28 iunii 1988, art. 62-65: AAS 80 (1988) 876-877; cf. S. CONGR. PRO CULT. DIV., Ep. ad Praesides Conf. Episc. «*De normis servandis quoad libros liturgicos in vulgus edendos, illorum translatione in linguas hodiernas peracta*», diei 25 octobris 1973, n. 1: AAS 66 (1974) 98.

104. For the good of the faithful, the Holy See reserves to itself the right to prepare translations in any language, and to approve them for liturgical use.[74] Nevertheless, even if the Apostolic See, by means of the Congregation for Divine Worship and the Discipline of the Sacraments, may intervene from time to time out of necessity in the preparation of translations, it still belongs to the competent Conference of Bishops to approve their assumption into liturgical use within the boundaries of a given ecclesiastical territory, unless otherwise explicitly indicated in the decree of approbation of the translation promulgated by the Apostolic See. Afterwards, for the purpose of obtaining the *recognitio* of the Holy See, the Conference shall transmit the decree of approbation for its territory together with the text itself, in accordance with the norms of this Instruction and of the other requirements of the law.

105. For reasons such as those set forth in nn. 76 and 84 above or for other urgent reasons of pastoral need, commissions, councils, committees, or work groups depending directly on the Apostolic See are established by decree of the Congregation for Divine Worship and the Discipline of the Sacraments for the purpose of working on the translation either of individual liturgical books or of several. In this case,

---

74 *Code of Canon Law*, cann. 333, 360; Pope John Paul II, Apost. Const. *Pastor Bonus*, 28 June 1988, art. 62-65: AAS 80 (1988) 876-877; cf. S. Congr. for Divine Worship, Letter to the Presidents of the Conferences of Bishops *De normis servandis quoad libros liturgicos in vulgus edendos, illorum translatione in linguas hodiernas peracta*, 25 October 1973, n. 1: AAS 66 (1974) 98.

in casu, in quantum fieri potest, consultabuntur aliqui saltem ex Episcopis, ad quos res pertinet.

6. De novis textibus liturgicis in lingua vulgari conficiendis

106. Circa compositionem novorum textuum liturgicorum, linguis vulgaribus conficiendorum, qui fortasse iis ex editionibus typicis latinis translatis addantur, normae iam vigentes observentur, peculiariter illae, quae in Instructione *«Varietates legitimae»* continentur.[75] Singularis Conferentia Episcoporum unam aut plures Commissiones instituat ad textus conficiendos aut ad studium ponendum in apta textuum accommodatione, qui textus recognitionis causa ad Congregationem de Cultu Divino et Disciplina Sacramentorum transmittantur, antequam quibusvis libris edantur, usui celebrantium et generatim christifidelium destinatis.[76]

107. Animo perpendendum est compositionem novorum textuum precationum aut rubricarum non spectare ad se ut ad finem proprium, sed eo consilio suscipi debere, ut peculiari necessitati culturali aut pastorali occurratur. Quapropter hoc est stricte officium Commissionum liturgicarum localium et nationalium, non autem Commissionum, de quibus supra ad nn. 92-104 est

---

75 Cf. CONGR. DE CULT. DIV. ET DISC. SACR., Instr. *Varietates legitimae*, diei 25 ianuarii 1994: AAS 87 (1995) 288-314.

76 Cf. *ibidem*, n. 36: AAS 87 (1995) 302.

insofar as possible, at least some of the Bishops involved in the matter will be consulted.

6. The composition of new liturgical texts in a vernacular language

106. Regarding the composition of new liturgical texts prepared in vernacular languages, which may perhaps be added to those translated from the Latin *editiones typicae*, the norms currently in force are to be observed, in particular those contained in the Instruction *Varietates legitimae*.[75] An individual Conference of Bishops shall establish one or more Commissions for the preparation of texts or for the work involved in the suitable adaptation of texts. The texts are then to be sent to the Congregation for Divine Worship and the Discipline of the Sacraments for the *recognitio*, prior to the publication of any books intended for the celebrants or for the general use of the Christian faithful.[76]

107. It is to be borne in mind that the composition of new texts of prayers or rubrics is not an end in itself, but must be undertaken for the purpose of meeting a particular cultural or pastoral need. For this reason it is strictly the task of the local and national liturgical Commissions, and not of the Commissions treated in nn. 92-104 above. New texts

---

75 Cf. Congr. for Divine Worship and the Discipline of the Sacraments, Instr. *Varietates legitimae*, 25 January 1994: AAS 87 (1995) 288-314.

76 Cf. *ibid.*, n. 36: AAS 87 (1995) 302.

dictum. Textus novi, lingua vulgari compositi, sicut aliae accommodationes legitime inductae nihil contineant repugnans muneri, significationi, structurae, stylo, argumento theologico aut tradito thesauro vocabulorum neque aliis magni momenti qualitatibus textuum, quae in editionibus typicis inveniuntur.[77]

108. Cantus et hymni liturgici peculiaris momenti et efficacitatis sunt. Praesertim dominica, «die Domini», cantus populi fidelis ad celebrationem sacrae Missae congregati, non minus quam orationibus, lectionibus et homilia, ratione authentica nuntium afferant Liturgiae, dum sensum communis fidei et communionis in caritate fovent.[78] Si a popolo fideli diffusius adhibentur, satis sint stabiles, ita ut confusio in populo vitetur. Intra quinquennium ab editione huius Instructionis computandos, Conferentiae Episcoporum, necessariam operam conferentibus Commissionibus nationalibus aut dioecesanis ad quas pertinet, aliisque peritis, edendum curent directorium seu repertorium textuum cantui liturgico destinatorum. Eiusmodi repertorium transmittatur, necessariae recognitionis causa, ad Congregationem de Cultu Divino et Disciplina Sacramentorum.

---

77 Cf. MISSALE ROMANUM, editio typica tertia: *Institutio Generalis*, n. 398.

78 IOANNES PAULUS PP. II, Litt. Ap. *Dies Domini*, diei 31 maii 1998, nn. 40, 50: AAS 90 (1998) 738, 745.

composed in a vernacular language, just as the other adaptations legitimately introduced, are to contain nothing that is inconsistent with the function, meaning, structure, style, theological content, traditional vocabulary or other important qualities of the texts found in the *editiones typicae*.[77]

108. Sung texts and liturgical hymns have a particular importance and efficacy. Especially on Sunday, the "Day of the Lord," the singing of the faithful gathered for the celebration of Holy Mass, no less than the prayers, the readings and the homily, express in an authentic way the message of the Liturgy while fostering a sense of common faith and communion in charity.[78] If they are used widely by the faithful, they should remain relatively fixed so that confusion among the people may be avoided. Within five years from the publication of this Instruction, the Conferences of Bishops, necessarily in collaboration with the national and diocesan Commissions and with other experts, shall provide for the publication of a directory or repertory of texts intended for liturgical singing. This document shall be transmitted for the necessary *recognitio* to the Congregation for Divine Worship and the Discipline of the Sacraments.

---

77 Cf. Missale Romanum, editio typica tertia: *Institutio Generalis*, n. 398.

78 Pope John Paul II, Apost. Letter *Dies Domini*, 31 May 1998, nn. 40, 50: AAS 90 (1998) 738, 745.

IV. De Librorum Liturgicorum Editione

109. Librorum liturgicorum Ritus romani, tantummodo textum latinum praebentium, ea dicitur *«editio typica»*, quae ex decreto Congregationis pro tempore competentis edita sit.[79] Editiones typicae publici iuris factae ante hanc Instructionem Typis Polyglottis Vaticanis vel a «Libreria Editrice Vaticana» divulgabantur; in posterum vero illae erunt de more Typis imprimendae Vaticanis, iure eas divulgandi praedictae «Libreria Editrice Vaticana» reservata.

110. Normae huius Instructionis, quoad omnia iura, se referunt ad editiones typicas editas vel edendas sive de integro libro, sive de eius parte agatur: editiones nempe Missalis Romani, Ordinis Missae, Lectionarii Missalis Romani, Evangeliarii Missalis Romani, Missalis parvi e Missali Romano et Lectionario excerpti, Passionis Domini Nostri Iesu Christi, Liturgiae Horarum, Ritualis Romani, Pontificalis Romani, Martyrologii Romani, Collectionis Missarum et Lectionarii de Beata Maria Virgine, Gradualis Romani, Antiphonalis Romani, necnon aliorum librorum cantus gregoriani, atque editiones librorum Ritus romani tamquam editiones typicas per decretum promulgatas, uti v. gr. sunt Caeremoniale Episcoporum et Calendarium Romanum.

---

79   Cf. *Codex Iuris Canonici*, can. 838 §2.

IV. The Publication of Liturgical Books

109. Of the liturgical books of the Roman Rite containing only Latin texts, only the one published by decree of the Congregation having competency at the time is designated the "*editio typica*."[79] The *editiones typicae* published prior to this Instruction were issued either *Typis Polyglottis Vaticanis* or by the *Libreria Editrice Vaticana*; in the future, they are usually to be printed by the *Tipografia Vaticana*, while the right of publication is reserved to the *Libreria Editrice Vaticana*.

110. The norms of this Instruction, as regards all rights, refer to the *editiones typicae* that have been or will be published, whether of a whole book or of a part: namely, the editions of the *Missale Romanum*, the *Ordo Missae*, the Lectionary of the *Missale Romanum*, the Evangeliary of the *Missale Romanum*, the *Missale parvum* extracted from the *Missale Romanum* and *Lectionarium*, the *Passio Domini Nostri Iesu Christi*, the *Liturgia Horarum*, the *Rituale Romanum*, the *Pontificale Romanum*, the *Martyrologium Romanum*, the *Collectio Missarum de Beata Maria Virgine* and its Lectionary, the *Graduale Romanum*, the *Antiphonale Romanum*, as well as the other books of Gregorian chant and the editions of the books of the Roman Rite promulgated by decree as *editiones typicae*, such as the *Caeremoniale Episcoporum* and the *Calendarium Romanum*.

---

79 Cf. *Code of Canon Law*, can. 838 § 2.

111. Quoad libros liturgicos Ritus romani editione typica promulgatos sive ante sive post Concilium Vaticanum II ex decreto Congregationum pro tempore competentium, Sedes Apostolica per Administrationem Patrimonii aut, eius nomine et mandato, per «Libreria Editrice Vaticana» ius proprietatis, quod vulgo dicitur «copyright», obtinet ac sibi vindicat. Licentia tamen denuo imprimendi ad Congregationem de Cultu Divino et Disciplina Sacramentorum spectat.

112. Librorum liturgicorum Ritus romani editiones «iuxta typicam» dicuntur, si agitur de libris lingua latina exaratis qui ex concessione Congregationis de Cultu Divino et Disciplina Sacramentorum ab editore post editionem typicam parantur.

113. Ad editiones «iuxta typicam», usui liturgico destinatas, quod attinet: ius libros liturgicos excudendi, qui unum textum latinum referunt, reservatur ad «Libreria Editrice Vaticana» atque iis editoribus, quibus Congregatio de Cultu Divino et Disciplina Sacramentorum concredere maluit expressis pactionibus, nisi aliud constet ex normis in ipsa editione typica insertis.

114. Ius libros liturgicos Ritus romani lingua vernacula transferendi vel saltem ad usum liturgicum rite approbandi, atque eos edendi seu typis evulgandi in proprio territorio

111. As regards the liturgical books of the Roman Rite promulgated in an *editio typica* either before or after the Second Vatican Council by decree of the Congregations competent at the time, the Apostolic See, through the *Administratio Patrimonii* or, in its name and by its mandate, through the Libreria Editrice Vaticana, possesses and reserves to itself the right of ownership commonly known as "copyright." The granting of permission for a reprinting pertains to the Congregation for Divine Worship and the Discipline of the Sacraments.

112. Of the liturgical books of the Roman Rite, those prepared in the Latin language by an editor after the publication of the *editio typica*, with the permission of the Congregation for Divine Worship and the Discipline of the Sacraments, are said to be "*iuxta typicam.*"

113. As regards the editions *iuxta typicam* intended for liturgical use: the right of printing liturgical books containing only the Latin text is reserved to the *Libreria Editrice Vaticana* and to those editors to whom the Congregation for Divine Worship and the Discipline of the Sacraments will have chosen to grant contracts, unless a different provision is made in the norms inserted into the editio typica itself.

114. The right of translating the liturgical books of the Roman Rite in a vernacular language, or at least the right of approving them for liturgical use and of printing and publishing them in their own territory, remains uniquely that

unice apud Conferentiam Episcoporum permanet,
attentis tamen iuribus et recognitionis[80] et proprietatis
Sedis Apostolicae, etiam hac in Instructione expositis.

115. Quoad libros vero liturgicos edendos, qui, in linguam
vernaculam translati, proprii sunt cuiusdam Conferentiae
Episcoporum, ius editionis reservatur editoribus, quibus
id Conferentia Episcoporum expressis pactionibus tributum
sit, ratione habita tum praescriptorum legis civilis tum
consuetudinum iuridicarum in unaquaque natione vigentium
pro libris edendis.

116. Ut editor ad editiones «iuxta typicam» usui liturgico
destinatas imprimendas procedere possit, debet:

a. si agitur de libris tantummodo textum latinum
    praebentibus, singulis vicibus licentiam obtinere
    a Congregatione de Cultu Divino et Disciplina
    Sacramentorum, deinde cum Administratione
    Patrimonii Sedis Apostolicae aut cum «Libreria
    Editrice Vaticana», quae nomine et mandato
    eiusdem Administrationis aget, conventionem
    inire de condicionibus ad publicam horum librorum
    divulgationem spectantibus;

b. si agitur de libris textum lingua vernacula exaratum
    praebentibus, iuxta rerum adiuncta, licentiam obtinere
    a Praeside Conferentiae Episcoporum vel Instituti seu

---

80 Cf. *ibidem*, can. 838 §3.

of the Conference of Bishops, with due regard, however,
to the rights of *recognitio*[80] and the proprietary rights of the
Apostolic See, also set forth in this Instruction.

115. As regards the publication of liturgical books translated
into the vernacular which are the property of a given Conference of Bishops, the right of publication is reserved to
those editors to whom the Conference of Bishops shall have
given this right by contract, with due regard for the requirements both of civil law and of juridical custom prevailing in
each country for the publication of books.

116. In order for an editor to be able to proceed to the
printing of editions *iuxta typicam* intended for liturgical use,
he must do the following:

a. in the case of books containing only the Latin text,
    obtain, in each single instance, the consent of the
    Congregation for Divine Worship and the Discipline of
    the Sacraments, and then enter into an agreement with
    the *Administratio Patrimonii Sedis Apostolicae* or with the
    Libreria Editrice Vaticana, which acts in the name and
    by the mandate of the same body, regarding the condi-
    tions for the publication of such books;

b. in the case of books containing texts in a vernacular
    language, obtain the consent, according to the circum-
    stances, of the President of the Conference of Bishops,

---

80   Cf. *ibid.*, can. 838 § 3.

Commissionis, qui de Sanctae Sedis licentia plurium
Conferentiarum nomine res gerit, simulque cum eo de
condicionibus pro publica horum librorum divulgatione
conventionem inire, attentis normis et legibus in propria
natione vigentibus;

c. si agitur de libris qui praesertim textum popularem
    referunt sed etiam diffuse textum latinum praebent,
    pro ista parte latina omnia ad normam n. 116a fiant.

117. Iura editionis ac proprietatis ad omnes translationes
textuum liturgicorum spectantia, aut saltem iura legis
civilis, quae necessaria sunt ad plenam libertatem pollendam
in textibus publici iuris faciendis vel corrigendis, penes
Conferentias Episcoporum aut earum Commissiones liturgicas
nationales maneant.[81] Idem institutum fruatur iure consilia
capiendi necessaria ad praecavendum et emendandum usum
improprium textuum.

118. Ubi ius proprietatis de textibus liturgicis in linguam
popularem translatis commune sit pluribus Conferentiis
Episcoporum, forma licentiae singulis Conferentiis
concedendae, in quantum fieri potest, sic exaretur, ut res
a singulis ipsis Conferentiis administrentur, ad normam
iuris. Sin secus, coetus quidem ad hoc administrandum ab
Apostolica Sede erigetur, collatis consiliis cum Episcopis.

---

81 S. CONGR. PRO CULT. DIV., Declaratio, diei 15 maii 1970: *Notitiae* 6 (1970) 153.

the Institute or the Commission that manages the matter in the name of several Conferences by license of the Holy See, and enter at the same time into an agreement with this body regarding the conditions for publication of such books, with due regard for the norms and laws in force in that country;

c. in the case of books containing principally a vernacular text but also containing extensive use of the Latin text, the norms of n. 116a are to be observed for the Latin part.

117. The rights of publication and the copyright for all translations of liturgical books, or at least the rights in civil law necessary for exercising complete liberty in publishing or correcting texts, is to remain with the Conferences of Bishops or their national liturgical Commissions.[81] The same body shall possess the right of taking any measures necessary to prevent or correct any improper use of the texts.

118. Wherever the copyright for translated liturgical texts is common to several Conferences, a licensing agreement is to be prepared for the individual Conferences, such that, insofar as possible, the matter may be administered by the individual Conferences themselves, according to the norm of law. Otherwise, a body shall be established for such administration by the Apostolic See, after consultation with the Bishops.

---

81 S. Congr. for Divine Worship, Decl., 15 May 1970: *Notitiae* 6 (1970) 153.

119. Concordantia librorum liturgicorum cum editionibus typicis approbatis pro usu liturgico, si agitur de textu solummodo lingua latina exarato, constare debet ex attestatione Congregationis de Cultu Divino et Disciplina Sacramentorum; si autem agitur de textu lingua vernacula exarato vel de casu ut supra, ad n. 116c, expositum, constare debet ex attestatione Ordinarii loci in quo libri publici iuris fiunt.[82]

120. Libri, quorum ope textus liturgici cum populo vel pro eodem lingua vulgari proferuntur, ea sint dignitate insignes ut species exterior libri ipsa fideles ad maiorem reverentiam verbi Dei rerumque sacrarum inducat.[83] Idcirco necessarium est ut, quam primum fieri possit, gradus ad tempus institutus superetur, cuius propria sunt foliola et fasciculi in unum collecti, ubicumque habentur. Omnes libri, usui liturgico destinati sacerdotum celebrantium vel diaconorum, magnitudine sint sufficienter ampla, ita ut a libris distinguantur ad usum personalem fidelium spectantibus. In iis nimius vitetur luxus, qui necessarie sumptus afferret, aliquibus immodicos. Pictura linearis involucri et imagines pictae in paginis libri item nobilem quandam simplicitatem prae se ferant atque inductionem eorum solummodo stylorum, qui in contextu culturali vim perennem atque universalem attrahendi habeant.

---

82 Cf. *Codex Iuris Canonici*, can. 826 §2; cf. etiam infra, n. 111.

83 Cf. CONC. OECUM. VAT. II, Const. *Sacrosanctum Concilium*, n. 122; S. RITUUM CONGR., Instr. *Inter Oecumenici*, n. 40e: AAS 56 (1964) 886.

119. The correspondence of the liturgical books with the *editiones typicae* approved for liturgical use, in the case of a text prepared only in the Latin language, must be established by the attestation of the Congregation for Divine Worship and the Discipline of the Sacraments; however, in the case of a text prepared in a vernacular language or in the case described above, in n. 116c, it must be established by attestation of the local Ordinary in whose diocese the books are published.[82]

120. The books from which the liturgical texts are recited in the vernacular with or on behalf of the people should be marked by such a dignity that the exterior appearance of the book itself will lead the faithful to a greater reverence for the word of God and for sacred realities.[83] Thus it is necessary as soon as possible to move beyond the temporary phase characterized by leaflets or fascicles, wherever these exist. All books intended for the liturgical use of priest or deacon celebrants are to be of a size sufficient to distinguish them from the books intended for the personal use of the faithful. To be avoided in them is any extravagance which would necessarily lead to costs that would be unaffordable for some. Pictures or images on the cover and in the pages of the book should be characterized by a certain noble simplicity and by the use of only those styles that have a universal and perennial appeal in the cultural context.

---

82   Cf. *Code of Canon Law*, can. 826 § 2; cf. also below, n. 111.

83   Cf. Second Vatican Council, Const. *Sacrosanctum Concilium*, n. 122; S. Congr. of Rites, Instr. *Inter Oecumenici*, n. 40e: AAS 56 (1964) 886.

121. Etiam in subsidiis pastoralibus pro privato usu fidelium edendis, quae participationem in actionibus liturgicis foveant, editores attendere debent ad iura proprietatis:

a. Sanctae Sedis, si agitur de textu latino, vel de musica gregoriana in libris cantus edita sive ante sive post Concilium Vaticanum II, iis tamen exceptis quae in usum omnium concessa sunt vel in futurum concedentur;

b. unius Conferentiae Episcoporum vel plurium simul Conferentiarum Episcoporum, si agitur de textu lingua vernacula exarato et de musica in eodem textu impressa et quae sit propria Conferentiae vel Conferentiarum.

Ad haec subsidia, praesertim si in forma librorum eduntur, extendi debet licentia Episcopi dioecesani, ad normam iuris.[84]

122. Invigilandum est optioni inter editores efficiendae, quibus impressio per typos librorum liturgicorum committatur, eos excludendo, quorum libri editi non prompte cognoscantur conformari ad spiritum et normas traditionis catholicae.

---

84 *Codex Iuris Canonici*, can. 826 §3.

121. Even in the case of pastoral aids published for the private use of the faithful and intended to foster their participation in the liturgical celebrations, the publishers must observe the proprietary rights:

a. of the Holy See, in the case of the Latin text, or of the Gregorian music in books of chant published either before or after the Second Vatican Council—with the exception, however, of those rights conceded universally, or those to be thus conceded in the future;

b. of the Conference of Bishops or of several Conferences of Bishops simultaneously, in the case of a text prepared in a vernacular language or of the music printed in the same text, which is the property of the Conference or Conferences.

For these aids, especially if published in the form of books, the consent of the diocesan Bishop is required, according to the norm of law.[84]

122. Care is to be taken to ensure that the choice of publishers for the printing of the liturgical books be made in such a way as to exclude any whose publications are not readily seen to conform to the spirit and norms of Catholic tradition.

---

84 *Code of Canon Law*, can. 826 § 3.

123. Quoad textus vi conventionis cum Ecclesiis particularibus et communitatibus ecclesialibus a plena communione Sanctae Sedis seiunctis effectae, oportet plena et legitima iura Episcoporum catholicorum et Apostolicae Sedis serventur inducendi quasvis mutationes et correctiones quae necessariae reputantur ad eius usum inter catholicos.

124. Secundum iudicium Conferentiae Episcoporum, libelli vel tabellae pro usu fidelium textus liturgicos complectentes, excipi possunt a regula generali qua libri liturgici lingua vulgari exarati omnia continere debent, quae in textu typico latino seu editione typica habentur. Quoad editiones autem officiales, nempe ad usum liturgicum sacerdotis, diaconi vel competentis ministri laici, serventur ea quae supra, ad nn. 66-69 dicuntur.[85]

125. Praeter ea, quae in editione typica continentur vel providentur aut singillatim exposita sunt in hac Instructione, nullus textus addatur editioni vulgari, nisi praecedat approbatio a Congregatione de Cultu Divino et Disciplina Sacramentorum concessa.

---

85 Cf. CONC. OECUM. VAT. II, Const. *Sacrosanctum Concilium*, n. 63b; S. CONGR. DE CULT. DIV., Declaratio «*De interpretationibus popularibus novorum textuum liturgicorum*», diei 15 septembris 1969: *Notitiae* 5 (1969) 333-334.

123. Regarding texts produced by agreement with the particular Churches and ecclesial communities separated from the communion of the Holy See, it is necessary that the Catholic Bishops and the Apostolic See retain full rights for introducing any changes or corrections that may be deemed necessary for their use among Catholics.

124. According to the judgment of the Conference of Bishops, leaflets or cards containing liturgical texts for the use of the faithful may be excepted from the general rule by which liturgical books prepared in a vernacular language must contain everything that is in the Latin *textus typicus* or *editio typica*. As for the official editions, namely those for the liturgical use of the priest, deacon or competent lay minister, the norms mentioned above, in nn. 66-69, are to be maintained.[85]

125. Besides what is contained in the editio typica or foreseen or set forth specifically in this Instruction, no text is to be added in the vernacular edition without prior approbation granted by the Congregation for Divine Worship and the Discipline of the Sacraments.

---

85 Second Vatican Council, Const. *Sacrosanctum Concilium*, n. 63b; S. Congr. for Divine Worship, Decl. *De interpretationibus popularibus novorum textuum liturgicorum*, 15 September 1969: *Notitiae* 5 (1969) 333-334.

V. De Translatione Textuum
Propriorum Liturgicorum

1. De Propriis dioecesium

126. In translatione textuum ut typicorum a Sede Apostolica approbatorum Proprii liturgici dioecesium conficienda, haec quae sequuntur sunt observanda:

a. Translatio fiat a Commissione liturgica dioecesana[86] aut alia ab Episcopo dioecesano ad hoc instituta et deinde ab Episcopo dioecesano approbari debet, consilio capto cleri atque in re peritorum;

b. Translatio, recognitionis causa, proponatur Congregationi de Cultu Divino et Disciplina Sacramentorum, tribus exemplaribus textus typici una cum translatione missis;

c. Relatio insuper exaretur, quae contineat oportet:

    i. decretum, quo a Sede Apostolica textus typicus approbatus est,

    ii. rationes seu criteria in translatione observata,

---

86 Cf. Pius PP. XII, Litt. Enc. *Mediator Dei*, diei 20 novembris 1947: AAS 39 (1947) 561-562; Conc. Oecum. Vat. II, Const. *Sacrosanctum Concilium*, n. 45.

V. The Translation of Proper Liturgical Texts

1. Diocesan propers

126. In the preparation of a translation of texts of a diocesan liturgical approved by the Apostolic See as *textus typici*, the following are to be observed:

a. The translation is to be done by the diocesan liturgical Commission[86] or by another body designated by the diocesan Bishop for this purpose, and then it must be approved by the diocesan Bishop, after consultation with his clergy and with experts;

b. The translation is to be sent to the Congregation for Divine Worship and the Discipline of the Sacraments for the *recognitio*, along with three copies of the *textus typicus* together with the translation;

c. A *relatio* is to be prepared as well, which is to contain:

    i. the decree by which the *textus typicus* has been approved by the Apostolic See,

    ii. the process and criteria followed in the translation;

---

86 Cf. Pope Pius XII, Encycl. Letter *Mediator Dei*, 20 November 1947: AAS 39 (1947) 561-562; Second Vatican Council, Const. *Sacrosanctum Concilium*, n. 45.

iii. elenchus personarum, quae variis in gradibus rei participarunt, una cum brevi descriptione experientiae vel facultatum atque notarum academicarum, quae illis sunt propriae;

d. Cum de linguis agitur minus late diffusis, Conferentia Episcoporum testificari debet textum esse accurate translatum in linguam, ad quam res pertinet, ut supra, ad n. 86.

127. In textibus typis excussis exhibeantur decreta, per quae translationibus concessa est recognitio Sanctae Sedis, aut saltem recognitio concessa memoretur, additis die, mense, anno et numero protocolli decreti a Dicasterio emanati, eisdem servatis normis ut supra, ad n. 68. Duo exemplaria textuum typis editorum ad Congregationem de Cultu Divino et Disciplina Sacramentorum transmittantur.

2. De Propriis familiarum religiosarum
128. In translatione textuum ut typicorum a Sede Apostolica approbatorum Proprii liturgici familiae religiosae conficienda, id est Instituti vitae consecratae vel Societatis vitae apostolicae aut alius associationis vel coetus approbati iure illa habendi fruentis, haec, quae sequuntur, sunt observanda:

a. Translatio fiat a Commissione generali liturgica aut ab alia ad hoc constituta a Moderatore Supremo vel saltem

iii. a list of the persons who have participated at
various stages of the work, together with a brief
description of their experience or abilities, and
of their academic degrees;

d. In the case of the less widely diffused languages, the
Conference of Bishops should testify that the text is
accurately translated into the language in question,
as mentioned above, in n. 86.

127. In the printed text are to be contained the decrees by
means of which the *recognitio* of the Holy See is granted for
the translations; or at least a mention is to be made of the
recognitio, including the date, the month, the year, and the
protocol number of the decree published by the Dicastery, in
keeping with the same norms as above, in n. 68. Two copies
of the printed text are to be sent to the Congregation for
Divine Worship and the Discipline of the Sacraments.

2. Propers of religious families

128. In the preparation the translation of texts approved by
the Apostolic See as *textus typici* for religious families, that is,
Institutes of Consecrated Life or Societies of Apostolic Life,
or other approved associations or organizations having the
rights to their use, the following are to be observed:

a. The translation is to be made by the general liturgical
Commission or by another body constituted for the
purpose by the Supreme Moderator or at least by his

de eius mandato Superiori Provinciali dato, et deinde a Moderatore Supremo cum voto deliberativo eius Consilii approbanda est, consilio, pro opportunitate, capto peritorum et sodalium idoneorum Instituti vel Societatis;

b. Translatio, recognitionis causa, proponatur Congregationi de Cultu Divino et Disciplina Sacramentorum, tribus exemplaribus textus typici una cum translatione missis;

c. Relatio insuper exaretur, quae contineat oportet:

    i. decretum, quo a Sede Apostolica textus typicus approbatus est,

    ii. rationes seu criteria in translatione observata,

    iii. elenchus personarum, quae variis in gradibus rei participarunt, una cum brevi descriptione experientiae vel facultatum atque notarum academicarum, quae illis sunt propriae;

d. Cum de linguis agitur minus late diffusis, Conferentia Episcoporum testificari debet textum esse accurate translatum in linguam, ad quam res pertinet, ut supra, ad n. 86;

mandate given to the Provincial Superior, and then it is to be approved by the Supreme Moderator with the deliberative vote of his Council, after any necessary consultation with experts and with appropriate members of the Institute or Society;

b. The translation is to be sent to the Congregation for Divine Worship and the Discipline of the Sacraments for the *recognitio*, together with three copies of the *textus typicus*;

c. A *relatio* is also to be prepared, which is to contain:

    i.   the decree by which the *textus typicus* has been approved by the Apostolic See,

    ii. the process and criteria followed in the translation,

    iii. a list of the persons who have participated at various stages of the work, together with a brief description of their experience or abilities, and of their academic degrees;

d. In the case of the less widely diffused languages, the Conference of Bishops should testify that the text is accurately translated into the language in question, as mentioned above, in n. 86;

e.   Circa familias religiosas iuris dioecesani eadem
    ratio procedendi servetur, praeterquam quod textus
    ab Episcopo dioecesano, una cum iudicio suae
    approbationis mittendus, est ad Congregationem
    de Cultu Divino et Disciplina Sacramentorum.

129. In Propriis liturgicis familiarum religiosarum, translatio
Sacrorum Bibliorum ad usum liturgicum eadem lingua pro
eodem territorio ad normam iuris approbata adhibeatur. Si
hoc difficile evadit, res ad Congregationem de Cultu Divino
et Disciplina Sacramentorum remittatur.

130. In textibus typis excussis exhibeantur decreta, per quae
translationibus concessa est recognitio Sanctae Sedis, aut
saltem recognitio concessa memoretur, additis die, mense,
anno et numero protocolli decreti a Dicasterio emanati,
eisdem servatis normis ut supra, ad n. 68. Duo exemplaria
textuum typis editorum ad Congregationem de Cultu Divino
et Disciplina Sacramentorum transmittantur.

Conclusio

131. Approbatio tempore praeterito singillatim concessa
translationibus liturgicis non desinit vigere, licet principium
vel criterium sit adhibitum, quod ab iis differt, quae in
hac Instructione continentur. A die tamen, quo haec

e. As regards religious families of diocesan right, the same
    procedure is to be followed, but in addition, the text
    is to be sent by the diocesan Bishop, together with
    his judgment of approbation, to the Congregation for
    Divine Worship and the Discipline of the Sacraments.

129. In the liturgical Propers of religious families, the translation of the Sacred Scriptures to be employed for liturgical use
is to be the same one approved for liturgical use according to
the norm of law for the same territory. If this proves difficult,
the matter is to be referred to the Congregation for Divine
Worship and the Discipline of the Sacraments.

130. In the printed text are to be contained the decrees by
means of which the *recognitio* of the Holy See is granted for
the translations, or at least a mention is to be made of the
recognitio, including the date, the month, the year, and the
protocol number of the decree published by the Dicastery, in
keeping with the same norms as above, in n. 68. Two copies
of the printed text are to be sent to the Congregation for
Divine Worship and the Discipline of the Sacraments.

Conclusion

131. Approbation granted in the past for individual liturgical
translations remains in effect even if a principle or criterion
has been followed which differs from those contained in
this Instruction. Nevertheless, from the day on which this

Instructio publici iuris facta est, novum temporis spatium coepit initium quoad emendationes efficiendas, aut considerationes denuo disceptandas de sermonibus seu idiomatibus vulgaribus in usum liturgicum inducendis, necnon translationes vulgari sermone iam hucusque confectas recognoscendas.

132. Intra quinquennium a die, quo haec Instructio publici iuris facta est, Praesides Conferentiarum Episcoporum et Supremi Moderatores familiarum religiosarum et institutorum eiusdem iuris praesentare tenentur Congregationi de Cultu Divino et Disciplina Sacramentorum integram agendi rationem circa libros liturgicos, in cuiusque territorio vel instituto, vulgari sermone redditos.

133. Insuper normae hac Instructione statutae vim totam consequantur ad translationes, quae iam habentur, emendandas, atque praecaveatur ne huiusmodi emendationes ulterius procrastinentur. Novus hic nisus, ut speratur, momentum stabilitatis habebit in vita Ecclesiae, adeo ut firmum fundamentum comparetur, in quo navitas liturgica populi Dei nitatur atque impensa afferatur renovatio catechesis.

Instruction is published, a new period begins for the making of emendations or for undertaking anew the consideration of the introduction of vernacular languages or idioms into liturgical use, as well as for revising translations heretofore made into vernacular languages.

132. Within five years from the date of publication of this Instruction, the Presidents of the Conferences of Bishops and the Supreme Moderators of religious families and institutes equivalent in law are bound to present to the Congregation for Divine Worship and the Discipline of the Sacraments an integral plan regarding the liturgical books translated into the vernacular in their respective territories or institutes.

133. In addition, the norms established by this Instruction attain full force for the emendation of previous translations, and any further delay in making such emendations is to be avoided. It is to be hoped that this new effort will provide stability in the life of the Church, so as to lay a firm foundation for supporting the liturgical life of God's people and bringing about a solid renewal of catechesis.

Hanc Instructionem, quae de mandato Summi Pontificis, litteris
Em.mi Cardinalis Secretarii Status die 1 mensis februarii anno
1997datis (Prot. n.408.304), a Congregatione de Cultu Divino
et Disciplina Sacramentorum exarata est, ipse Summus Pontifex
Ioannes Paulus II, in audientia die 20 mensis martii anno 2001
Em.mo Domino Cardinali Secretario Status concessa, approbavit
et auctoritate Sua confirmavit, mandans ut publici iuris fieret et
die 25 mensis aprilis eiusdem anni vigere inciperet.

Ex aedibus Congregationis de Cultu Divino et Disciplina
Sacramentorum, die 28 mensis martii anno 2001.

Georgius A. Card. Medina Estévez
Praefectus

† Franciscus Pius Tamburrino
Archiepiscopus a Secretis

After the preparation of this Instruction by the Congregation
for Divine Worship and the Discipline of the Sacraments in virtue
of the mandate of the Supreme Pontiff transmitted in a letter of
the Cardinal Secretary of State dated 1 February 1997 (Prot. n.
408.304), the same Supreme Pontiff, in an audience granted to
the Cardinal Secretary of State on 20 March 2001, approved
this Instruction and confirmed it by his own authority, ordering
that it be published, and that it enter into force on the 25th day
of April of the same year.

From the offices of the Congregation for Divine Worship and
the Discipline of the Sacraments, 28 March, the year 2001.

Jorge A. Card. Medina Estévez
Prefect

✝ Francesco Pio Tamburrino
Archbishop Secretary

APPENDIX A

PRESS RELEASE, MAY 7, 2001

❧

CONGREGATION FOR DIVINE WORSHIP AND
THE DISCIPLINE OF THE SACRAMENTS

Background

The Great Post-Conciliar Instructions
On 4 December 1963 the Fathers of the Second Vatican
Council approved the Constitution on the Sacred Liturgy,
Sacrosanctum Concilium. In order to facilitate the implementation of the liturgical renewal desired by the Council
Fathers, the Holy See has subsequently published five documents of special importance, each successively numbered as
an "Instruction for the Right Application of the Constitution
on the Sacred Liturgy of the Second Vatican Council."

The first of these, *Inter Oecumenici*, was issued by the Sacred
Congregation of Rites and the "Consilium" for the Implementation of the Liturgy Constitution on 26 September 1964, and
contained initial general principles for the orderly carrying
out of the liturgical renewal. Three years later, on 4 May
1967, a second Instruction was issued, *Tres abhinc annos*. This
described further adaptations to the Order of Mass. The third

Instruction, *Liturgicae instaurationes*, of 5 September 1970, was issued by the Sacred Congregation for Divine Worship, the body that succeeded the Sacred Congregation of Rites and the "Consilium." It provided directives on the central role of the Bishop in the renewal of the Liturgy throughout the diocese.

Subsequently the intensive activity of the revision of the Latin editions of the liturgical books and their translation into the various modern languages was the main vehicle for the liturgical renewal. After the general completion of this phase, there came a period of practical experience, which necessarily required a considerable space of time. With Pope John Paul II's Apostolic Letter *Vicesimus quintus annus*, issued on 4 December 1988 to mark the 25th anniversary of the Council's Constitution, there began a new gradual process of evaluation, completion and consolidation of the liturgical renewal. On 25 January 1994, the Congregation for Divine Worship and the Discipline of the Sacraments carried this process forward by issuing the Fourth "Instruction for the Right Application of the Constitution on the Sacred Liturgy of the Second Vatican Council," *Varietates legitimae*, concerning difficult questions on the Roman Liturgy and inculturation.

A Fifth Instruction
In February 1997 the Holy Father asked the Congregation for Divine Worship and the Discipline of the Sacraments to carry forward the process of the liturgical renewal by codifying the conclusions of its work in collaboration with the

Bishops over the years regarding the question of the liturgical translations. This matter had been in course, as mentioned, since 1988.

As a result, on 20 March 2001 the Fifth post-Conciliar "Instruction for the Right Application of the Constitution on the Sacred Liturgy" of the Second Vatican Council, *Liturgiam authenticam*, was approved by the Holy Father in an audience with the Cardinal Secretary of State and on 28 March it was issued by the Congregation for Divine Worship and the Discipline of the Sacraments. It takes effect on 25 April 2001.

The Instruction *Liturgiam authenticam* serves to set forth authoritatively the manner in which the provisions of article 36 of the Liturgy Constitution are to be applied to the vernacular translation of the texts of the Roman Liturgy. That article states:

§ 1. The use of the Latin language is to be preserved in the Latin Rites, while maintaining particular law.

§ 2. However, since the use of the vernacular not infre-quently may be of great benefit to the people either in the Mass or in the administration of the Sacraments, or in the other parts of the Liturgy, a wider use may be made of it especially in the readings and instructions [to the people], in certain prayers and sung texts, according to the norms on this matter to be set forth in detail in the chapters following.

§ 3. With due regard for such norms, it pertains to the competent territorial ecclesiastical authority mentioned in article 22, § 2, in consultation, if the case arises, with Bishops of neighboring regions which have the same language, to make decisions regarding whether and to what extent the vernacular language is to be used. Their decisions are to be approved—that is, confirmed—by the Apostolic See.

§ 4. A translation of a Latin text into the vernacular for use in the Liturgy must be approved by the competent territorial ecclesiastical authority mentioned above.

It should be mentioned that there have been a number of legal and other developments in the meantime, among them measures which have further defined the "competent territorial ecclesiastical authorities" of which the Constitution speaks. In practice these have become what are known as the Bishops' Conferences today.

Overview

The Fifth Instruction begins by referring to the initiative of the Council and the work of the successive Popes and the Bishops throughout the world, recalling the successes of the liturgical reform, while at the same time noting the continued vigilance needed in order to preserve the identity and unity of the Roman Rite throughout the world. In this regard, the Instruction takes up the observations made in 1988 by Pope

John Paul II calling for progress beyond an initial phase to one of improved translations of liturgical texts. Accordingly, *Liturgiam authenticam* offers the Latin Church a new formulation of principles of translation with the benefit of more than thirty years' experience in the use of the vernacular in liturgical celebrations.

Liturgiam authenticam supersedes all norms previously set forth on liturgical translation, with the exception of those in the fourth Instruction *Varietates legitimae*, and specifies that the two Instructions should be read in conjunction with each other. It calls more than once for a new era in translation of liturgical texts.

It should be noted that the new document substitutes for all previous norms while integrating much of their content, drawing them together in a more unified and systematic way, underpinning them with some careful reflection, and linking them to certain related questions that so far have been treated separately. Moreover, it is faced with the task of speaking in a few pages of principles applicable to several hundred languages currently used in liturgical celebration in every part of the world. It does not employ the technical terminology of linguistics or of the human sciences but refers principally to the domain of pastoral experience.

In what follows, the general development of the document is followed, but not always the exact wording or order of points.

Choice of Vernacular Languages

Only the more commonly spoken languages should be employed in the Liturgy, avoiding the introduction of too many languages for liturgical use, which could prove divisive by fragmenting a people into small groups. A number of factors should be kept in mind when choosing a language for liturgical use, such as the number of priests, deacons and lay collaborators at ease in a given tongue, the availability of translators for each language, and the practical possibility, including cost, of producing and publishing accurate translations of the liturgical books.

Dialects which do not have the backing of academic and cultural formation may not be formally accepted as liturgical languages, although they may be used for the Prayers of the Faithful, sung texts or parts of the homily.

The Instruction next gives a careful updated outline of the process to be followed by the Conferences of Bishops in communion with the Holy See in deciding up full or partial introduction into liturgical use of a given language.

The Translation of Liturgical Texts

The heart of the Instruction is a fresh exposition with a reflective tone of principles that should govern the vernacular translation of liturgical texts. From the outset this section stresses the sacred nature of the Liturgy, which the translated texts must carefully safeguard.

The Roman Rite, like all the great historical liturgical families of the Catholic Church, has its own style and structure that must be respected in so far as possible in translation. The Instruction repeats the call of earlier papal documents for an approach to the translation of liturgical texts that sees it not so much a work of creative inventiveness as one of fidelity and exactness in rendering the Latin texts into a vernacular language, with all due consideration for the particular way that each language has of expressing itself. The special needs that must be addressed when making translations intended for newly evangelized territories are mentioned, and the Instruction also discusses the conditions under which more significant adaptations of texts and rites may occur, referring the regulation of these issues to the Instruction *Varietates legitimae*.

Using Other Texts as Aids

The usefulness of consulting ancient source texts is acknowledged and encouraged, though it is noted that the text of the *editio typica*, the official modern Latin edition, is always the point of departure for the translation. When the Latin text employs certain words from other ancient languages (e.g., *alleluia*, *Amen*, or *Kyrie eleison*), such terms may be retained in their original languages. Liturgical translations are to be made only from the *editio typica* of the Latin and never from other translations in turn. The *Neo-Vulgate*, the current Catholic version of the Latin Bible, should be employed as an auxiliary tool in preparing biblical translations for use in the Liturgy.

Vocabulary

The vocabulary chosen for liturgical translation must be at one and the same time easily comprehensible to ordinary people and also expressive of the dignity and oratorical rhythm of the original: a language of praise and worship which fosters reverence and gratitude in the face of God's glory. The language of these texts is, therefore, not intended primarily as an expression of the inner dispositions of the faithful but rather of God's revealed word and his continual dialogue with his people in history.

Translations must be freed from exaggerated dependence on modern modes of expression and in general from psychologizing language. Even forms of speech deemed slightly archaic may on occasion be appropriate to the liturgical vocabulary.

The liturgical texts are neither completely autonomous nor separable from the general context of Christian life. There are in the Liturgy no texts that are intended to promote discriminatory or hostile attitudes to non-Catholic Christians, to the Jewish community or other religions, or which in any way deny universal equality in human dignity. If incorrect interpretation arises, the matter should be clarified, but this is not primarily the business of translations. The homily and catechesis are there to help fill out and explain their meaning and to clarify certain texts.

Gender

Many languages have nouns and pronouns capable of referring to both the masculine and the feminine in a single term.
The abandonment of these terms under pressure of criticism
on ideological or other grounds is not always wise or necessary nor is it an inevitable part of linguistic development.
Traditional collective terms should be retained in instances
where their loss would compromise a clear notion of man as
a unitary, inclusive and corporate yet truly personal figure, as
expressed, for example, by the Hebrew term *adam*, the Greek
anthropos or the Latin *homo*. Similarly, the expression of such
inclusivity may not be achieved by a quasi-mechanical
changes in grammatical number, or by the creation of pairs
of masculine and feminine terms.

The traditional grammatical gender of the persons of the
Trinity should be maintained. Expressions such as *Filius
hominis* (Son of Man) and *Patres* (fathers) are to be translated
with exactitude wherever found in biblical or liturgical texts.
The feminine pronoun must be retained in referring to the
Church. Kinship terms and the grammatical gender of angels,
demons and pagan deities should be translated, and their
gender retained, in light of the usage of the original text and
of the traditional usage of the modern language in question.

The Translation of a Text

Translations should try not to extend or to restrict the
meaning of the original terms, and terms that recall publicity
slogans or those that have political, ideological or similar

overtones should be avoided. Academic and secular style-books on vernacular composition should not be used uncritically, since the Church has distinctive things to say and a style of expression that is appropriate to them.

Translation is a collaborative effort that should maintain continuity as much as possible between the original and vernacular texts. The translator must possess not only special skills, but also a trust in divine mercy and a spirit of prayer, as well as a readiness to accept review of his work by others. When substantial changes are needed to bring a given liturgical book into conformity with this Instruction, such revisions must be made all at once so as to avoid repeated disturbances or a sense of continual instability in liturgical prayer.

Scriptural Translations
Special consideration is given to the translation of the Scriptures for use in the Liturgy. A version should be developed which is exegetically sound and also suitable for the Liturgy. Such a translation should be used universally within the area of a single Bishops' Conference and be the same for a given passage in all parts of the liturgical books. The aim should be a distinctive sacred style in each language that is consonant, as far as possible, with the established vocabulary of popular Catholic usage and major catechetical texts. All doubtful cases regarding canonicity and the ordering of verses should be resolved by reference to the Neo-Vulgate.

Concrete images found in words referring in figurative language that speaks, for example of the "finger," the "hand," the "face" of God, or of his "walking," and terms like "flesh" and the so on, should usually be translated literally and not replaced by abstractions. These are distinctive features of the biblical text that are to be maintained.

Other Liturgical Texts
Norms for the translation of the Bible as used in the Liturgy apply also in general to the translation of liturgical prayers. At the same time, it must be acknowledged that while liturgical prayer is formed by the culture which practices it, it is also formative of culture, so that the relationship is not merely passive. As a result, liturgical language can be expected to diverge from ordinary speech, as well as to reflect its better elements. The ideal is to develop a dignified vernacular fit for worship in a given cultural context.

Liturgical vocabulary must include the major characteristics of the Roman Rite, and should be drawn from patristic sources and harmonized with biblical texts. The vocabulary and usage of the vernacular translation of the *Catechism of the Catholic Church* should be respected as far as this is feasible, and the proper distinctive terms should be used for sacred persons or things, rather than employing the same words as for the persons or things of everyday domestic life.

Syntax, style and literary genre are also key elements to be considered in rendering a faithful translation. The relationship between clauses, especially as expressed through subordination and devices such as parallelism, must be accurately conveyed. Verbs must be translated precisely in respect of person, number and voice, while some latitude will be needed in rendering more complex syntactical structures.

A prime consideration should be the fact that liturgical texts are intended to be publicly proclaimed aloud and even sung.

Particular Types of Texts
Specific norms are then given for the translation of Eucharistic Prayers, the Creed, (which is to be translated in the first person singular: "I believe . . ."), and the general ordering and layout of liturgical books and their preliminary decrees and introductory texts. This is followed by a description of the preparation of translations by Bishops' Conferences and the processes to be used for obtaining the approval and confirmation of liturgical texts from the Holy See. The present special requirements of papal approbation for sacramental formulae are reaffirmed, as is the insistence on the desirability of a single translation of the Liturgy, especially the Order of Mass, within each language group.

The Organization of Translation Work and Commissions
The preparation of translations is a serious charge incumbent in the first place upon the Bishops themselves, even if they naturally often draw on the services of experts. In all work of translation at least some of the Bishops should be closely involved, not only personally checking the final texts, but

taking active part in the various stages of preparation. Even if not all the Bishops of a Conference are proficient in a given language used within its territory, they must take collegial responsibility for the liturgical texts and the overall pastoral language policy.

The Instruction sets out clearly the procedures (in general those in use until now) for the approval of texts by the Bishops and the forwarding of the texts for review and confirmation by the Congregation for Divine Worship. The document devotes some space to expressing the significance of the referral of liturgical matters to the Holy See, in terms partly based on the Pope John Paul II's Motu Proprio *Apostolos suos* of 1998, in which the nature and function of Bishops' Conferences was clarified. The referral procedure is a sign of the Bishops' communion with the Pope and a means to strengthening it. It is also a guarantee of the quality of texts and aims at ensuring that the liturgical celebrations of the particular Churches (dioceses) be in full harmony with the tradition of the Catholic Church down through the ages and throughout the world.

Where cooperation is appropriate or necessary between Bishops' Conferences using the same language, the Congregation for Divine Worship and the Discipline of the Sacraments alone erects joint or "mixed" commissions, usually following up on a request from the Bishops. Such commissions are not autonomous and are not a channel of communication between the Holy See and the Bishops'

Conferences. They have no decision-making capacity, but are solely at the service of the pastoral office of the Bishops. They are concerned exclusively with the translation of the Latin *editiones typicae*, not with the composition of new vernacular texts, nor the consideration of theoretical questions or cultural adaptations; and the establishment of relations with similar bodies of other language groups lies outside their competence.

The Fifth Instruction recommends that at least some of the Bishops making up the commission be chairmen of the liturgical commission of their Bishops' Conference. In any case the "mixed" commission is run by Bishops, in accordance with statutes confirmed by the Congregation for Divine Worship. These statutes should normally have the approval of all participating Bishops' Conferences, but if this is not feasible, the Congregation for Divine Worship may both draw up and approve statutes on its own authority.

Commissions of this kind, says the document, operate best by coordinating use of resources available to individual Bishops' Conferences, so that one Conference, for example, may produce a first draft of a translation which is subsequently refined by the other Conferences of Bishops to arrive at an improved and universally serviceable text.

Such "mixed" commissions are not intended to replace national and diocesan liturgical commissions and therefore cannot take on any of the functions of the latter.

Because of the importance of the work, all involved in the activity of a "mixed" commission on a stable basis, other than the Bishops, must obtain a *nihil obstat* from the Congregation for Divine Worship and the Discipline of the Sacraments prior to taking up their duties. Like all connected with the commission, they serve only for a fixed term and are bound by a contract to confidentiality and anonymity in completing assignments.

Existing commissions must bring their statutes into conformity with this Instruction and submit them to the Congregation for Divine Worship within two years from the issue date of the Instruction.

The document also stresses the Holy See's own need for liturgical translations, especially in the major world languages, and its desire to be more closely involved in their preparation in future. It also refers in general terms to various kinds of bodies which the Congregation for Divine Worship may set up to resolve translation problems of one or more languages.

New Compositions
A section on the composition of new texts notes that their purpose is solely to respond to genuine cultural and pastoral needs. As such, their composition is the exclusive province of Bishops' Conferences rather than the "mixed" translation commissions. They are to respect the style, structure, vocabulary and other traditional qualities of the Roman Rite. Particularly important, because of their impact on the person

and on the memory, are hymns and chants. There is to be a general review of vernacular material in this field and Bishops' Conferences are to regulate the question with the assent of the Congregation within five years.

The Instruction concludes with a number of brief technical sections giving guidelines on publication of editions of liturgical books, including copyright, and on procedures for the translation of the liturgical texts proper to individual dioceses and religious communities.

APPENDIX B

VARIETATES LEGITIMAE: FOURTH INSTRUCTION ON THE ROMAN LITURGY AND INCULTURATION

⤜⤏

CONGREGATION FOR DIVINE WORSHIP AND
THE DISCIPLINE OF THE SACRAMENTS

Introduction

1. Legitimate differences in the Roman rite were allowed in the past and were foreseen by the Second Vatican Council in the Constitution on the Sacred Liturgy *Sacrosanctum Concilium*, especially in the Missions.[1] "Even in the liturgy the Church has no wish to impose a rigid uniformity in matters that do not affect the faith or the good of the whole community."[2] It has known and still knows many different

---

1   Cf. Vatican Council II, Constitution *Sacrosanctum Concilium*, n. 38; cf. also n. 40, 3.

2   *Ibid.*, n. 37.

forms and liturgical families, and considers that this diversity, far from harming her unity, underlines its value.[3]

2. In his Apostolic Letter *Vicesimus quintus annus*, the Holy Father Pope John Paul II described the attempt to make the liturgy take root in different cultures as an important task for liturgical renewal.[4] This work was foreseen in earlier Instructions and in liturgical books, and it must be followed up in the light of experience, welcoming, where necessary, cultural values "which are compatible with the true and authentic spirit of the liturgy, always respecting the substantial unity of the Roman rite as expressed in the liturgical books."[5]

A. Nature of This Instruction

3. By order of the Supreme Pontiff, the Congregation for Divine Worship and the Discipline of the Sacraments has prepared this Instruction: The *Norms for the adaptation of the liturgy to the temperament and conditions of different peoples,* which were given in articles 37-40 of the Constitution *Sacrosanctum Concilium*, are here defined; certain principles, expressed in general terms in those articles, are explained

---

3   Cf. Vatican Council II, Decree *Orientalium Ecclesiarum*, n. 2; Constitution *Sacrosanctum Concilium*, nn. 3 and 4; *Catechism of the Catholic Church*, nn. 1200-1206, especially nn. 1204-1206.

4   Cf. John Paul II, Apostolic Letter *Vicesimus quintus annus*, 4 December 1988, n. 16: *Acta Apostolicae Sedis* (AAS) 81 (1989), 912.

5   *Ibid.*

more precisely, the directives are set out in a more appropriate way and the order to be followed is clearly set out, so that in future this will be considered the only correct procedure. Since the theological principles relating to questions of faith and inculturation have still to be examined in depth, this Congregation wishes to help bishops and Episcopal Conferences to consider or put into effect, according to the law, such adaptations as are already foreseen in the liturgical books; to re-examine critically arrangements that have already been made; and if, in certain cultures, pastoral need requires that form of adaptation of the liturgy which the Constitution calls "more profound" and at the same time considers "more difficult," to make arrangements for putting it into effect in accordance with the law.

B. Preliminary Observations

4. The Constitution *Sacrosanctum Concilium* spoke of the different forms of liturgical adaptation.[6] Subsequently the Magisterium of the Church has used the term "inculturation" to define more precisely "the incarnation of the Gospel in autonomous cultures and at the same time the introduction of these cultures into the life of the Church."[7] Inculturation signifies "an intimate transformation of the authentic cultural

---

6   Cf. Vatican Council II, Constitution *Sacrosanctum Concilium*, nn. 37-40.

7   John Paul II, Encyclical Letter *Slavorum Apostoli*, 2 June 1985, n. 21: AAS 77 (1985), 802-803; Discourse to the Plenary Assembly of the Pontifical Council for Culture, 17 January 1987, n. 5: AAS 79 (1987), 1204-1205.

values by their integration into Christianity and the implantation of Christianity into different human cultures."[8]

The change of vocabulary is understandable, even in the liturgical sphere. The expression "adaptation," taken from missionary terminology, could lead one to think of modifications of a somewhat transitory and external nature.[9] The term "inculturation" is a better expression to designate a double movement: "By inculturation, the Church makes the Gospel incarnate in different cultures, and at the same time introduces peoples, together with their cultures, into her own community."[10] On the one hand the penetration of the Gospel into a given sociocultural milieu "gives inner fruitfulness to the spiritual qualities and gifts proper to each people . . . , strengthens these qualities, perfects them and restores them in Christ."[11]

On the other hand, the Church assimilates these values, when they are compatible with the Gospel, "to deepen

---

8   John Paul II, Encyclical Letter *Redemptoris missio*, 7 December 1990, n. 52: AAS 83 (1991), 300.

9   Cf. *ibid.* and Synod of Bishops, Final Report *Exeunte coetu secundo*, 7 December 1985, D 4.

10   John Paul II, Encyclical Letter *Redemptoris missio*, 7 December 1990, n. 52: AAS 83 (1991), 300.

11   Vatican Council II, Pastoral Constitution *Gaudium et spes*, n. 58.

understanding of Christ's message and give it more effective expression in the liturgy and in the many different aspects of the life of the community of believers."[12] This double move-ment in the work of inculturation thus expresses one of the component elements of the mystery of the Incarnation.[13]

5. Inculturation thus understood has its place in worship as in other areas of the life of the Church.[14] It constitutes one of the aspects of the inculturation of the Gospel, which calls for true integration,[15] in the life of faith of each people, of the permanent values of a culture, rather than their transient expressions. It must, then, be in full solidarity with a much greater action, a unified pastoral strategy which takes account

---

12   *Ibid.*

13   Cf. John Paul II, Apostolic Exhortation *Catechesi tradendae*, 16 October 1979, n. 53: AAS 71 (1979), 1319.

14   Cf. *Code of Canon Law of the Oriental Churches*, can. 584 § 2: *"Evangelizatio gentium ita fiat, ut servata integritate fidei et morum Evangelium se in cultura singulorum populorum exprimere possit, in catechesi scilicet, in ritibus propriis liturgicis, in arte sacra, in iure particulari ac demum in tota vita ecclesiali."*

15   Cf. John Paul II, Apostolic Exhortation *Catechesi tradendae*, 16 October 1979, n. 53: AAS 71 (1979), 1320: ". . . concerning evangelization in general, we can say that it is a call to bring the strength of the Gospel to the heart of culture and cultures. . . . It is in this way that it can propose to cultures the knowledge of the mystery hidden and help them to make of their own living tradition original expressions of life, celebration and Christian thought."

of the human situation.[16] As in all forms of the work of evangelization, this patient and complex undertaking calls for methodical research and ongoing discernment.[17] The inculturation of the Christian life and of liturgical celebrations must be the fruit of a progressive maturity in the faith of the people.[18]

6. The present instruction has different situations in view. There are in the first place those countries which do not have a Christian tradition or where the Gospel has been proclaimed in modern times by missionaries who brought the Roman rite with them. It is now more evident that "coming into contact with different cultures, the church

---

16 Cf. John Paul II, Encyclical Letter *Redemptoris missio*, 7 December 1990, n. 52: AAS 83 (1991), 300: "Inculturation is a slow process covering the whole of missionary life and involves all who are active in the mission '*ad gentes*,' and Christian communities in the measure that they are developing." Discourse to the Plenary Assembly of the Pontifical Council for Culture, 17 January 1987: AAS 79 (1987), 1205: "I strongly reaffirm the need to mobilize the whole church into a creative effort toward a renewed evangelization of both people and cultures. It is only by a joint effort that the church will be able to bring the hope of Christ into the heart of cultures and present-day ways of thinking."

17 Cf. Pontifical Biblical Commission, *Foi et culture a la lumiere de la Bible*, 1981; and International Theological Commission Document on Faith and Inculturation, *Commissio theologica*, 1988.

18 Cf. John Paul II, Discourse to the Bishops of Zaire, 12 April 1983, n. 5: AAS 75 (1983), 620: "How is it that a faith which has truly matured, is deep and firm, does not succeed in expressing itself in a language, in a catechesis, in theological reflection, in prayer, in the liturgy, in art, in the institutions which are truly related to the African soul of your compatriots? There is the key to the important and complex question of the liturgy, to mention just one area. Satisfactory progress in this domain can only be the fruit of a progressive growth in faith, linked with spiritual discernment, theological clarity, a sense of the universal church."

must welcome all that can be reconciled with the Gospel in the tradition of a people to bring to it the riches of Christ and to be enriched in turn by the many different forms of wisdom of the nations of the earth."[19]

7. The situation is different in the countries with a long-standing Western Christian tradition, where the culture has already been penetrated for a long time by the faith and the liturgy expressed in the Roman rite. That has helped the welcome given to liturgical reform in these countries, and the measures of adaptation envisaged in the liturgical books were considered, on the whole, sufficient to allow for legitimate local diversity (cf. below nos. 53-61). In some countries, however, where several cultures coexist, especially as a result of immigration, it is necessary to take account of the particular problems which this poses (cf. below no. 49).

8. It is necessary to be equally attentive to the progressive growth both in countries with a Christian tradition and in others of a culture marked by indifference or disinterest in religion.[20] In the face of this situation, it is not so much a

---

19 John Paul II, Discourse to the Plenary Assembly of the Pontifical Council for Culture, 17 January 1987, n. 5: AAS 79 (1987), 1204: "In coming into contact with the cultures, the church must welcome all that in the traditions of peoples is compatible with the Gospel, to give all the riches of Christ to them and to enrich itself of the varied wisdom of the nations of the earth."

20 Cf. John Paul II, Discourse to the Plenary Assembly of the Pontifical Council for Culture, 17 January 1987, n. 5: AAS 79 (1987), 1205; cf. also Apostolic Letter *Vicesimus quintus annus*, 4 December 1988, n. 17: AAS 81 (1989), 913-914.

matter of inculturation, which assumes that there are pre-existent religious values and evangelizes them; but rather a matter of insisting on liturgical formation[21] and finding the most suitable means to reach spirits and hearts.

I. Process of Inculturation Throughout the History of Salvation

9. Light is shed upon the problems being posed about the inculturation of the Roman rite in the history of salvation. The process of inculturation was a process which developed in many ways.

The people of Israel throughout its history preserved the certain knowledge that it was the chosen people of God, the witness of his action and love in the midst of the nations. It took from neighboring peoples certain forms of worship, but its faith in the God of Abraham, Isaac and Jacob subjected these borrowings to profound modifications, principally changes of significance but also often changes in the form, as it incorporated these elements into its religious practice, in order to celebrate the memory of God's wonderful deeds in its history.

The encounter between the Jewish world and Greek wisdom gave rise to a new form of inculturation: the translation of

---

21   Cf. Vatican Council II, Constitution *Sacrosanctum Concilium*, nn. 19 and 35, 3.

the Bible into Greek introduced the word of God into a world that had been closed to it and caused, under divine inspiration, an enrichment of the Scriptures.

10. "The law of Moses, the prophets and the psalms" (cf. Lk 24:27 and 44) was a preparation for the coming of the Son of God upon earth. The Old Testament, comprising the life and culture of the people of Israel, is also the history of salvation.

On coming to the earth the Son of God, "born of a woman, born under the law" (Gal 4:4), associated himself with social and cultural conditions of the people of the Alliance with whom he lived and prayed.[22] In becoming a man he became a member of a people, a country and an epoch "and in a certain way, he thereby united himself to the whole human race."[23] For "we are all one in Christ, and the common nature of our humanity takes life in him. It is for this that he was called the 'New Adam.'"[24]

11. Christ, who wanted to share our human condition (cf. Heb 2:14), died for all in order to gather into unity the scattered children of God (cf. Jn 11:52). By his death he wanted to break down the wall of separation between mankind, to make Israel and the nations one people. By the power of his

---

22 Cf. Vatican Council II, Decree *Ad gentes*, n. 10.

23 Vatican Council II, Pastoral Constitution *Gaudium et spes*, n. 22.

24 St. Cyril of Alexandria, *In Ioannem*, I, 14: *Patrologia Graeca* (PG) 73, 162C.

resurrection he drew all people to himself and created out of them a single New Man (cf. Eph 2:14-16; Jn 12:32). In him a new world has been born (cf. 2 Cor 5:16-17) and everyone can become a new creature. In him, darkness has given place to light, promise became reality and all the religious aspirations of humanity found their fulfillment. By the offering that he made of his body, once for all (cf. Heb 10:10), Christ Jesus brought about the fullness of worship in spirit and in truth in the renewal which he wished for his disciples (cf. Jn 4:23-24).

12. "In Christ . . . the fullness of divine worship has come to us."[25] In him we have the High Priest, taken from among men (cf. Heb 5:1-5, 10:19-21), put to death in the flesh but brought to life in the spirit (cf. 1 Pt 3:18). As Christ and Lord, he has made out of the new people "a kingdom of priests for God his Father" (cf. Rev 1:6, 5:9-10).[26] But before inaugurating by the shedding of his blood the Paschal Mystery,[27] which constitutes the essential element of Christian worship,[28] Christ wanted to institute the Eucharist, the memorial of his death and resurrection, until he comes again. Here

---

25 Vatican Council II, Constitution *Sacrosanctum Concilium*, n. 5.

26 Cf. Vatican Council II, Dogmatic Constitution *Lumen gentium*, n. 10.

27 Cf. *Missale Romanum*, Fifth Weekday of the Passion of the Lord, 5: Prayer One: ". . . *per suum cruorem instituit paschale mysterium.*"

28 Cf. Paul VI, Apostolic Letter *Mysterii paschalis*, 14 February 1969: AAS 61 (1969), 222-226.

is to be found the fundamental principle of Christian liturgy and the kernel of its ritual expression.

13. At the moment of his going to his Father, the risen Christ assures his disciples of his presence and sends them to proclaim the Gospel to the whole of creation, to make disciples of all nations and baptize them (cf. Mt 28:15; Mk 16:15; Acts 1:8). On the day of Pentecost, the coming of the Holy Spirit created a new community within the human race, uniting all, in spite of the differences of language, which were a sign of division (cf. Acts 2:1-11). Henceforth the wonders of God will be made known to people of every language and culture (cf. Acts 10:44-48). Those redeemed by the blood of the Lamb and united in fraternal communion (cf. Acts 2:42) are called from "every tribe, language, people and nation" (cf. Rev 5:9).

14. Faith in Christ offers to all nations the possibility of being beneficiaries of the promise and of sharing in the heritage of the people of the covenant (cf. Eph 3:6), without renouncing their culture. Under the inspiration of the Holy Spirit, following the example of St. Peter (cf. Acts 10), St. Paul opened the doors of the Church, not keeping the Gospel within the restrictions of the Mosaic law but keeping what he himself had received of the tradition which came from the Lord (cf. 1 Cor 11:23). Thus, from the beginning, the Church did not demand of converts who were uncircumcised "anything beyond what was necessary" according to the decision of the apostolic assembly of Jerusalem (cf. Acts 15:28).

15. In gathering together to break the bread on the first day of the week, which became the day of the Lord (cf. Acts 20:7; Rev 1:10), the first Christian communities followed the command of Jesus who, in the context of the memorial of the Jewish pasch, instituted the memorial of his Passion. In continuity with the unique history of salvation, they spontaneously took the forms and texts of Jewish worship and adapted them to express the radical newness of Christian worship.[29] Under the guidance of the Holy Spirit, discernment was exercised between what could be kept and what was to be discarded of the Jewish heritage of worship.

16. The spread of the Gospel in the world gave rise to other types of ritual in the Churches coming from the Gentiles, under the influence of different cultural traditions. Under the constant guidance of the Holy Spirit, discernment was exercised to distinguish those elements coming from "pagan" cultures which were incompatible with Christianity from those which could be accepted in harmony with Apostolic tradition and in fidelity to the Gospel of salvation.

17. The creation and the development of the forms of Christian celebration developed gradually according to local conditions, in the great cultural areas where the Good News was proclaimed. Thus were born distinct liturgical families of the Churches of the West and of the East. Their rich patrimony preserves faithfully the Christian tradition in its

---

29 Cf. *Catechism of the Catholic Church*, n. 1096.

fullness.[30] The Church of the West has sometimes drawn elements of its liturgy from the patrimony of the liturgical families of the East.[31] The Church of Rome adopted in its liturgy the living language of the people, first Greek and then Latin, and, like other Latin Churches, accepted into its worship important events of social life and gave them a Christian significance. During the course of the centuries, the Roman rite has known how to integrate texts, chants, gestures and rites from various sources[32] and to adapt itself in local cultures in mission territories,[33] even if at certain periods a desire for liturgical uniformity obscured this fact.

18. In our own time, the Second Vatican Council recalled that the Church "fosters and assumes the ability, resources and customs of each people. In assuming them, the Church purifies, strengthens and ennobles them. . . . Whatever good lies latent in the religious practices and cultures of diverse

---

30 Cf. *ibid.*, nn. 1200-1203.

31 Cf. Vatican Council II, Decree *Unitatis redintegratio*, nn. 14-15.

32 Texts: cf. the sources of the prayers, the prefaces and the eucharistic prayers of the Roman Missal; Chants: for example the antiphons for 1 January, Baptism of the Lord; 8 September, the Improperia of Good Friday, the hymns of the Liturgy of the Hours; Gestures: for example the sprinkling of holy water, use of incense, genuflection, hands joined; Rites: for example Palm Sunday procession, the adoration of the Cross on Good Friday, the rogations.

33 Cf. St. Gregory the Great, *Letter to Mellitus*: Reg. XI, 59: CCL 140A, 961- 962; John VIII, Bull *Industriae tuae*, 26 June 880: PL 126, 904; Congregation for the Propagation of the Faith, Instruction to the Apostolic Vicars of China and Indochina (1654): *Collectanea S.C. de Propaganda Fide*, I, 1, Rome, 1907, n. 135; Instruction *Plane compertum*, 8 December 1939: AAS 32 (1940), 24-26.

peoples, it is not only saved from destruction but it is also cleansed, raised up, and made perfect unto the glory of God, the confounding of the devil, and the happiness of mankind."[34] So the liturgy of the Church must not be foreign to any country, people, or individual, and at the same time it should transcend the particularity of race and nation. It must be capable of expressing itself in every human culture, all the while maintaining its identity through fidelity to the tradition which comes to it from the Lord.[35]

19. The liturgy, like the Gospel, must respect cultures, but at the same time invite them to purify and sanctify themselves.

In adhering to Christ by faith, the Jews remained faithful to the Old Testament, which led to Jesus, the Messiah of Israel; they knew that he had fulfilled the Mosaic alliance, as the mediator of the new and eternal covenant, sealed in his blood on the cross. They knew that, by his one perfect sacrifice, he is the authentic High Priest and the definitive temple (cf. Heb 6-10), and the prescriptions of circumcision (cf. Gal 5:1-6), the Sabbath (cf. Mt 12:8 and similar),[36]

---

34 Vatican Council II, Dogmatic Constitution *Lumen gentium*, n. 17, also n. 13.

35 Cf. John Paul II, Apostolic Exhortation *Catechesi tradendae*, 16 October 1979, nn. 52-53: AAS 71 (1979), 1320-1321; Encyclical Letter *Redemptoris missio*, 7 December 1990, nn. 53-54: AAS 83 (1991), 300-302; *Catechism of the Catholic Church*, nn. 1204-1206.

36 Cf. also St. Ignatius of Antioch, *Letter to the Magnesians*, 9: Funk I, 199: "We have seen how former adherents of the ancient customs have since attained to a new hope; so that they have given up keeping the sabbath, and now order their lives by the Lord's day instead. . . ."

and the sacrifices of the temple (cf. Heb 10) became of only relative significance.

In a more radical way, Christians coming from paganism had to renounce idols, myths, superstitions (cf. Acts 19:18-19; 1 Cor 10:14-22, 2:20-22; 1 Jn 5:21) when they adhered to Christ.

But whatever their ethnic or cultural origin, Christians have to recognize the promise, the prophecy and the history of their salvation in the history of Israel. They must accept as the Word of God the books of the Old Testament as well as those of the New.[37] They welcome the sacramental signs, which can only be understood fully in the context of Holy Scripture and the life of the Church.[38]

20. The challenge which faced the first Christians, whether they came from the chosen people or from a pagan background, was to reconcile the renunciations demanded by faith in Christ with fidelity to the culture and traditions of the people to which they belonged.

---

37 Cf. Vatican Council II, Dogmatic Constitution *Dei Verbum*, nn. 14-16; *Ordo Lectionum Missae*, ed. typica altera, Praenotanda, n. 5: "It is the same mystery of Christ that the church announces when she proclaims the Old and New Testament in the celebration of the liturgy. The New Testament is, indeed, hidden in the Old and, in the New the Old is revealed. Because Christ is the center and fullness of all Scripture, as also of the whole liturgical celebration"; *Catechism of the Catholic Church*, nn. 120-123, 128-130, 1093-1095.

38 Cf. *Catechism of the Catholic Church*, nn. 1093-1096.

And so it will be for Christians of all times, as the words of St. Paul affirm: "We proclaim Christ crucified, scandal for the Jews, foolishness for the pagans" (1 Cor 1:23).

The discernment exercised during the course of the Church's history remains necessary, so that through the liturgy the work of salvation accomplished by Christ may continue faithfully in the Church by the power of the Spirit, in different countries and times and in different human cultures.

II. The Requirements and Preliminary Conditions for Liturgical Inculturation

A. Requirements Emerging from the Nature of the Liturgy

21. Before any research on inculturation begins, it is necessary to keep in mind the nature of the liturgy. It "is, in fact the privileged place where Christians meet God and the one whom he has sent, Jesus Christ" (cf. Jn 17:3).[39] It is at once the action of Christ the priest and the action of the Church which is his body, because in order to accomplish his work of glorifying God and sanctifying mankind, achieved through visible signs, he always associates with himself the Church,

---

39 John Paul II, Apostolic Letter *Vicesimus quintus annus*, 4 December 1988, n. 7: AAS 81 (1989), 903-904.

which, through him and in the Holy Spirit, gives the Father the worship which is pleasing to him.[40]

22. The nature of the liturgy is intimately linked up with the nature of the Church; indeed, it is above all in the liturgy that the nature of the Church is manifested.[41] Now the Church has specific characteristics which distinguish it from every other assembly and community.

It is not gathered together by a human decision, but is called by God in the Holy Spirit and responds in faith to his gratuitous call ("*ekklesia*" derives from "*klesis*," "call"). This singular characteristic of the Church is revealed by its coming together as a priestly people, especially on the Lord's day, by the word which God addresses to his people and by the ministry of the priest who through the sacrament of orders acts in the person of Christ the Head.[42]

Because it is catholic, the Church overcomes the barriers which divide humanity: by Baptism all become children of God and form in Christ Jesus one people where "there is neither Jew nor Greek, neither slave nor free, neither male nor female" (Gal 3:28). Thus Church is called to gather all peoples, to speak the languages, to penetrate all cultures.

---

40   Cf. Vatican Council II, Constitution *Sacrosanctum Concilium*, nn. 5-7.

41   Cf. *ibid.*, n. 2; John Paul II, Apostolic Letter *Vicesimus quintus annus*, 4 December 1988, n. 9: AAS 81 (1989), 905-906.

42   Cf. Vatican Council II, Decree *Presbyterorum ordinis*, n. 2.

Finally, the Church is a pilgrim on the earth far from the Lord (cf. 2 Cor 5:6): It bears the marks of the present time in the sacraments and in its institutions, but is waiting in joyful hope for the coming of Jesus Christ (cf. Titus 2:13).[43] This is expressed in the prayers of petition: It shows that we are citizens of heaven (cf. Phil 3:20), at the same time attentive to the needs of mankind and of society (cf. 1 Tm 2:1-4).

23. The Church is nourished on the word of God written in the Old and New Testaments. When the Church proclaims the word in the liturgy, it welcomes it as a way in which Christ is present: "It is he who speaks when the Sacred Scriptures are read in Church."[44] For this reason the word of God is so important in the celebration of the liturgy[45] that the Holy Scripture must not be replaced by any other text, no matter how venerable it may be.[46] Likewise the Bible is

---

43 Cf. Vatican Council II, Dogmatic Constitution *Lumen gentium*, n. 48; Constitution *Sacrosanctum Concilium*, nn. 2 and 8.

44 Vatican Council II, Constitution *Sacrosanctum Concilium*, n. 7.

45 Cf. *ibid.*, n. 24.

46 Cf. *Ordo Lectionem Missae*, editio typica altera, Praenotanda, n. 12: "It is not allowed to suppress or reduce either the biblical readings in the celebration of Mass or the chants that are drawn from sacred Scripture. It is absolutely forbidden to replace these readings by other nonbiblical readings. It is through the word of God in the Scriptures that 'God continues to speak to his people' (*Sacrosanctum Concilium*, n. 33), and it is through familiarity with the Holy Scripture that the people of God, made docile by the Holy Spirit in the light of faith, can by their life and way of living witness to Christ before the whole world."

the indispensable source of the liturgy's language, of its signs, and of its prayer, especially in the psalms.[47]

24. Since the Church is the fruit of Christ's sacrifice, the liturgy is always the celebration of the Paschal Mystery of Christ, the glorification of God the Father and the sanctification of mankind by the power of the Holy Spirit.[48] Christian worship thus finds its most fundamental expression when every Sunday, throughout the whole world, Christians gather around the altar under the leadership of the priest, celebrate the Eucharist, listen to the word of God, and recall the death and resurrection of Christ, while awaiting his coming in glory.[49] Around this focal point, the Paschal Mystery is made present in different ways, in the celebration of each of the sacraments.

25. The whole life of the liturgy gravitates in the first place around the Eucharistic Sacrifice and the other sacraments given by Christ to his Church.[50] The Church has the duty to transmit them carefully and faithfully to every generation. In virtue of its pastoral authority, the Church can make dispositions to provide for the good of the faithful, according to

---

47   Cf. *Catechism of the Catholic Church*, nn. 2585-2589.

48   Cf. Vatican Council II, Constitution *Sacrosanctum Concilium*, n. 7.

49   Cf. *ibid.*, nn. 6, 47, 56, 102, 106; cf. *Missale Romanum*, Institutio Generalis, nn. 1, 7, 8.

50   Cf. Vatican Council II, Constitution *Sacrosanctum Concilium*, n. 6.

circumstances, times and places.[51] But it has no power over the things which are directly related to the will of Christ and which constitute the unchangeable part of the liturgy.[52] To break the link that the sacraments have with Christ who instituted them, and with the very beginnings of the Church,[53] would no longer be to inculturate them, but to empty them of their substance.

26. The Church of Christ is made present and signified, in a given place and in a given time, by the local or particular Churches, which through the liturgy reveals the Church in its true nature.[54] That is why every particular Church must be united with the universal Church not only in belief and sacramentals, but also in those practices received through

---

51   Cf. Council of Trent, Session 21, Chap. 2: Denz-Schonm. 1728; Vatican Council II, Constitution *Sacrosanctum Concilium*, nn. 48ff, 62ff.

52   Cf. Vatican Council II, Constitution *Sacrosanctum Concilium*, n. 21.

53   Cf. Sacred Congregation for the Doctrine of the Faith, Declaration *Inter Insigniores*, 15 October 1976: AAS 69 (1977), 107-108.

54   Cf. Vatican Council II, Dogmatic Constitution *Lumen gentium*, n. 28; cf. n. 26.

the Church as part of the uninterrupted apostolic tradition.[55] This includes, for example, daily prayer,[56] sanctification of Sunday and the rhythm of the week, the celebration of Easter and the unfolding of the mystery of Christ throughout the liturgical year,[57] the practice of penance and fasting,[58] the sacraments of Christian Initiation, the celebration of the memorial of the Lord and the relationship between the liturgy of the word and the Eucharistic liturgy, the forgiveness of sins, the ordained ministry, marriage, and the anointing of the sick.

27. In the liturgy the faith of the Church is expressed in a symbolic and communitarian form: This explains the need for a legislative framework for the organization of worship, the

---

55   Cf. St. Irenaeus, Against the Heresies, III, 2, 1-3; 3, 1-2: *Sources Chretiennes*, 211, 24-31; cf. St. Augustine, Letter to Januarius 54, 1: PL 33, 200: "But regarding those other observances which we keep and all the world keeps, and which do not derive from Scripture but from tradition, we are given to understand that they have been ordained or recommended to be kept by the apostles themselves or by the plenary councils, whose authority is well founded in the church"; cf. John Paul II, Encyclical Letter *Redemptoris missio*, 7 December 1990, nn. 53-54: AAS 83 (1991), 300-302; cf. Congregation for the Doctrine of the Faith, Letter to Bishops of the Catholic Church on Certain Aspects of the Church Understood as Communion, 28 May 1992, nn. 7-10.

56   Cf. Vatican Council II, Constitution *Sacrosanctum Concilium*, n. 83.

57   Cf. *ibid.*, nn. 102, 106 and appendix.

58   Cf. Paul VI, Apostolic Constitution *Paenitemini*, 17 February 1966: AAS 58 (1966), 177-198.

preparation of texts, and the celebration of rites.[59] The reason for the preceptive character of this legislation throughout the centuries and still today is to ensure the orthodoxy of worship: that is to say, not only to avoid errors, but also to pass on the faith in its integrity so that the "rule of prayer" (*lex orandi*) of the Church may correspond to "rule of faith" (*lex credendi*).[60]

However deep inculturation may go, the liturgy cannot do without legislation and vigilance on the part of those who have received this responsibility in the Church: the Apostolic See and, according to the prescriptions of the law, the Episcopal Conference for its territory and the bishop for his diocese.[61]

B. Preliminary Conditions for Inculturation of the Liturgy

28. The missionary tradition of the Church has always sought to evangelize people in their own language. Often indeed, it was the first apostles of a country who wrote down languages which up till then had only been oral. And this is

---

59 Cf. Vatican Council II, Constitution *Sacrosanctum Concilium*, nn. 22; 26; 28; 40, 3 and 128; *Code of Canon Law*, can. 2 and *passim*.

60 Cf. *Missale Romanum*, Institutio Generalis, Prooemium, n. 2; Paul VI, discourse to the Consilium for the Application of the Constitution on the Liturgy, 13 October 1966: AAS 58 (1966), 1146; 14 October 1968: AAS 60 (1968), 734.

61 Cf. Vatican Council II, Constitution *Sacrosanctum Concilium*, nn. 22; 36 §§ 3 and 4; 40, 1 and 2; 44-46; *Code of Canon Law*, cann. 447ff and 838.

right, as it is by the mother language, which conveys the mentality and the culture of a people, that one can reach the soul, mold it in the Christian spirit, and allow to share more deeply in the prayer of the Church.[62]

After the first evangelization, the proclamation of the word of God in the language of a country remains very useful for the people in their liturgical celebrations. The translation of the Bible, or at least of the biblical texts used in the liturgy, is the first necessary step in the process of the inculturation of the liturgy.[63]

So that the word of God may be received in a right and fruitful way, "it is necessary to foster a taste for Holy Scripture, as is witnessed by the ancient traditions of the rites of both East and West."[64] Thus inculturation of the liturgy presupposes the reception of the Sacred Scripture into a given culture.[65]

29. The different situations in which the Church finds itself are an important factor in judging the degree of liturgical

---

62 Cf. John Paul II, Encyclical Letter *Redemptoris missio*, 7 December 1990, n. 53: AAS 83 (1991), 300-302.

63 Cf. Vatican Council II, Constitution *Sacrosanctum Concilium*, nn. 35 and 36 §§ 2-3; *Code of Canon Law*, can. 825 § 1.

64 Cf. Vatican Council II, Constitution *Sacrosanctum Concilium*, n. 24.

65 Cf. *ibid.*; John Paul II, Apostolic Exhortation *Catechesi tradendae*, 16 October 1979, n. 55: AAS 71 (1979), 1322-1323.

inculturation that is necessary. The situation of countries that were evangelized centuries ago and where the Christian faith continues to influence the culture is different from countries which were evangelized more recently or where the Gospel has not penetrated deeply into cultural values.[66] Different again is the situation of a Church where Christians are a minority of the population. A more complex situation is found when the population has different languages and cultures. A precise evaluation of the situation is necessary in order to achieve satisfactory solutions.

30. To prepare an inculturation of the liturgy, Episcopal Conferences should call upon people who are competent both in the liturgical tradition of the Roman rite and in the appreciation of local cultural values. Preliminary studies of a historical, anthropological, exegetical and theological character are necessary. But these need to be examined in the light of the pastoral experience of the local clergy, especially those born in the country.[67] The advice of "wise people" of the country, whose human wisdom is enriched by the light of the Gospel, would also be valuable. Liturgical inculturation should try to satisfy the needs of traditional culture[68] and at the same time take account of the needs of those affected by an urban and industrial culture.

---

66 In the Constitution *Sacrosanctum Concilium* attention is drawn to nn. 38 and 40: "above all in the missions."

67 Cf. Vatican Council II, Decree *Ad gentes*, nn. 16 and 17.

68 Cf. *ibid.*, n. 19.

C. The Responsibility of the Episcopal Conference

31. Since it is a question of local culture, it is understandable that the Constitution *Sacrosanctum Concilium* assigned special responsibility in this matter to the "various kinds of competent territorial bodies of bishops legitimately established."[69] In regard to this, Episcopal Conferences must consider "carefully and prudently what elements taken from the traditions and cultures of individual peoples may properly be admitted into divine worship."[70] They can sometimes introduce "into the liturgy such elements as are not bound up with superstition and error . . . provided they are in keeping with the true and authentic spirit of the liturgy."[71]

32. Conferences may determine, according to the procedure given below (cf. nos. 62 and 65-69), whether the introduction into the liturgy of elements borrowed from the social and religious rites of a people, and which form a living part of their culture, will enrich their understanding of liturgical actions without producing negative effects on their faith and piety. They will always be careful to avoid the danger of introducing elements that might appear to the faithful as the return to a period before evangelization (cf. below, no. 47).

---

69   Vatican Council II, Constitution *Sacrosanctum Concilium*, n. 22 § 2; cf. *ibid.*, nn. 39 and 40, 1 and 2; *Code of Canon Law*, cann. 447-448ff.

70   Vatican Council II, Constitution *Sacrosanctum Concilium*, n. 40.

71   *Ibid.*, n. 37.

In any case, if changes in rites or texts are judged to be necessary, they must be harmonized with the rest of the liturgical life and, before being put into practice, still more before being made mandatory, they should first be presented to the clergy and then to the faithful in such a way as to avoid the danger of troubling them without good reason (cf. below, nos. 46 and 69).

III. Principles and Practical Norms for the Inculturation of the Roman Rite

33. As particular Churches, especially the young Churches, deepen their understanding of the liturgical heritage they have received from the Roman Church which gave them birth, they will be able in turn to find in their own cultural heritage appropriate forms, which can be integrated into the Roman rite where this is judged useful and necessary.

The liturgical formation of the faithful and the clergy, which is called for by the Constitution *Sacrosanctum Concilium*,[72] ought to help them to understand the meaning of the texts and the rites given in the present liturgical books. Often this will mean that elements which come from the tradition of the Roman rite do not have to be changed or suppressed.

---

72 Cf. *ibid.*, nn. 14-19.

A. General Principles

34. In the planning and execution of the inculturation of the Roman rite, the following points should be kept in mind: (1) the goal of inculturation; (2) the substantial unity of the Roman rite; (3) the competent authority.

35. The *goal* which should guide the inculturation of the Roman rite is that laid down by the Second Vatican Council as the basis of the general restoration of the liturgy: "Both texts and rites should be so drawn up that they express more clearly the holy things they signify and so that the Christian people, as far as possible, may be able to understand them with ease and to take part in the rites fully, actively and as befits a community."[73]

Rites also need "to be adapted to the capacity of the faithful and that there should not be a need for numerous explanations for them to be understood."[74] However, the nature of the liturgy always has to be borne in mind, as does the biblical and traditional character of its structure and the particular way in which it is expressed (cf. above, nos. 21-27).

36. The process of inculturation should maintain the *substantial unity* of the Roman rite.[75] This unity is currently expressed

---

73   *Ibid.*, n. 21.

74   Cf. *ibid.*, n. 34.

75   Cf. *ibid.*, nn. 37-40.

in the typical editions of liturgical books, published by authority of the Supreme Pontiff, and in the liturgical books approved by the Episcopal Conferences for their areas and confirmed by the Apostolic See.[76] The work of inculturation does not foresee the creation of new families of rites; inculturation responds to the needs of a particular culture and leads to adaptations which still remain part of the Roman rite.[77]

37. Adaptations of the Roman rite, even in the field of inculturation, depend completely on the authority of the Church. This authority belongs to the Apostolic See, which exercises it through the Congregation for Divine Worship and the Discipline of the Sacraments;[78] it also belongs, within the limits fixed by law, to Episcopal Conferences[79]

---

76 Cf. John Paul II, Apostolic Letter *Vicesimus quintus annus*, 4 December 1988, n. 16: AAS 81 (1989), 912.

77 Cf. John Paul II, Discourse to the Plenary Assembly of the Congregation for Divine Worship and the Discipline of the Sacraments, 26 January 1991, n. 3: AAS 83 (1991), 940: "This is not to suggest to the particular churches that they have a new task to undertake following the application of liturgical reform, that is to say, adaptation or inculturation. Nor is it intended to mean inculturation as the creation of alternative rites. . . . It is a question of collaborating so that the Roman rite, maintaining its own identity, may incorporate suitable adaptations."

78 Cf. Vatican Council II, Constitution *Sacrosanctum Concilium*, n. 22; *Code of Canon Law*, cann. 838 §§ 1 and 2; John Paul II, Apostolic Constitution *Pastor Bonus*, nn. 62, 64 § 3: AAS 80 (1988), 876-877; Apostolic Letter *Vicesimus quintus annus*, 4 December 1988, n. 19: AAS 81 (1989), 914-915.

79 Cf. Vatican Council II, Constitution *Sacrosanctum Concilium*, n. 22 § 2 and *Code of Canon Law*, cann. 447ff and 838 § 1 and 3; John Paul II, Apostolic Letter *Vicesimus quintus annus*, 4 December 1988, n. 20: AAS 81 (1989), 916.

and to the diocesan bishop.[80] "No other person, not even
if he is a priest, may on his own initiative add, remove, or
change anything in the liturgy."[81] Inculturation is not left
to the personal initiative of celebrants or to the collective
initiative of an assembly.[82]

Likewise concessions granted to one region cannot be
extended to other regions without the necessary authoriza-
tion, even if an Episcopal Conference considers that there are
sufficient reasons for adopting such measures in its own area.

B. Adaptations Which Can Be Made
38. In an analysis of a liturgical action with a view to its
inculturation, it is necessary to consider the traditional value
of the elements of the action and in particular their biblical

---

80   Cf. Vatican Council II, Constitution *Sacrosanctum Concilium*, n. 22 § 1 and *Code of
     Canon Law*, cann. 838 § 1 and 4; John Paul II, Apostolic Letter *Vicesimus quintus annus*,
     4 December 1988, n. 21: AAS 81 (1989), 916-917.

81   Cf. Vatican Council II, Constitution *Sacrosanctum Concilium*, n. 22 § 3.

82   The situation is different when, in the liturgical books published after the constitution,
     the introductions and the rubrics envisaged adaptations and the possibility of leaving a
     choice to the pastoral sensitivity of the one presiding, for example, when it says "if it is
     opportune," "in these or similar terms," "also," "according to circumstances," "either . . .
     or," "if convenient," "normally," "the most suitable form can be chosen." In making a
     choice, the celebrant should seek the good of the assembly, taking into account the spiri-
     tual preparation and mentality of the participants rather than his own preferences or the
     easiest solution. In celebrations for particular groups, other possibilities are available.
     Nonetheless, prudence and discretion are always called for in order to avoid the breaking
     up of the local church into little "churches" or "chapels" closed in upon themselves.

or patristic origin (cf. above, nos. 21-26), because it is not sufficient to distinguish between what can be changed and what is unchangeable.

39. *Language*, which is a means of communication between people. In liturgical celebrations its purpose is to announce to the faithful the good news of salvation[83] and to express the Church's prayer to the Lord. For this reason it must always express, along with the truths of the faith, the grandeur and holiness of the mysteries which are being celebrated.

Careful consideration therefore needs to be given to determine which elements in the language of the people can properly be introduced into liturgical celebrations, and in particular whether it is suitable or not to use expressions from non-Christian religions. It is just as important to take account of the different literary genres used in the liturgy: biblical texts, presidential prayers, psalmody, acclamations, refrains, responsories, hymns and litanies.

40. *Music* and *singing*, which express the soul of people, have pride of place in the liturgy. And so singing must be promoted, in the first place singing the liturgical text, so that the voices of the faithful may be heard in the liturgical

---

83   Cf. *Code of Canon Law*, cann. 762-772, especially 769.

actions themselves.[84] "In some parts of the world, especially mission lands, there are people who have their own musical traditions, and these play a great part in their religious and social life. Due importance is to be attached to their music and a suitable place given to it, not only in forming their attitude toward religion, but also in adapting worship to their native genius."[85]

It is important to note that a text which is sung is more deeply engraved in the memory than when it is read, which means that it is necessary to be demanding about the biblical and liturgical inspiration and the literary quality of texts which are meant to be sung.

Musical forms, melodies and musical instruments could be used in divine worship as long as they "are suitable, or can be made suitable, for sacred use, and provided they are in accord with the dignity of the place of worship, and truly contribute to the uplifting of the faithful."[86]

---

84 Cf. Vatican Council II, Constitution *Sacrosanctum Concilium*, n. 118; cf. also n. 54: While allowing that "a suitable place be allotted to the language of the country" in the chants, "steps should be taken so that the faithful may also be able to say or sign together in Latin those parts of the ordinary of the Mass which pertain to them," especially the Our Father, cf. *Missale Romanum*, Institutio Generalis, n. 19.

85 Vatican Council II, Constitution *Sacrosanctum Concilium*, n. 119.

86 *Ibid.*, n. 120.

41. The liturgy is an action, and so *gesture* and *posture* are especially important. Those which belong to the essential rites of the sacraments and which are required for their validity must be preserved just as they have been approved or determined by the supreme authority of the Church.[87]

The gestures and postures of the celebrating priest must express his special function: He presides over the assembly in the person of Christ.[88]

The gestures and postures of the assembly are signs of its unity and express its active participation and foster the spiritual attitude of the participants.[89] Each culture will choose those gestures and bodily postures which express the attitude of humanity before God, giving them a Christian significance, having some relationship, if possible, with the gestures and postures of the Bible.

42. Among some peoples, singing is instinctively accompanied by handclapping, rhythmic swaying and dance movements on the part of the participants. Such forms of external expression can have a place in the liturgical actions of these peoples, on condition that they are always the expression of

---

87 Cf. *Code of Canon Law*, can. 841.

88 Cf. Vatican Council II, Constitution *Sacrosanctum Concilium*, n. 33; *Code of Canon Law*, can. 899 § 2.

89 Cf. Vatican Council II, Constitution *Sacrosanctum Concilium*, n. 30.

true communal prayer of adoration, praise, offering and supplication, and not simply a performance.

43. The liturgical celebration is enriched by the presence of *art*, which helps the faithful to celebrate, meet God and pray. Art in the church, which is made up of all peoples and nations, should enjoy the freedom of expression, as long as it enhances the beauty of the buildings and liturgical rites, investing them with the respect and honor which is their due.[90] The arts should also be truly significant in the life and tradition of the people.

The same applies to the shape, location and decoration of the altar,[91] the place for the proclamation of the word of God[92] and for Baptism,[93] all the liturgical furnishings, vessels, vestments and colors.[94] Preference should be given to materials, forms and colors which are in use in the country.

44. The Constitution *Sacrosanctum Concilium* has firmly maintained the constant practice of the Church of encouraging the veneration by the faithful of images of Christ, the

---

90 Cf. *ibid.*, nn. 123-124; *Code of Canon Law*, can. 1216.

91 Cf. *Missale Romanum*, Institutio Generalis, nn. 259-270; *Code of Canon Law*, cann. 1235-1239, especially 1236.

92 Cf. *Missale Romanum*, Institutio Generalis, n. 272.

93 Cf. *De Benedictionibus*, Ordo benedictionis Baptisterii seu fontis baptismalis, nn. 832-837.

94 Cf. *Missale Romanum*, Institutio Generalis, nn. 287-310.

Virgin Mary and the Saints,[95] because the honor "given
to the image is given to its subject."[96] In different cultures
believers can be helped in their prayer and in their spiritual
life by seeing works of art which attempt, according to the
genius of the people, to express the divine mysteries.

45. Alongside liturgical celebrations and related to them, in
some particular Churches there are various manifestations
of popular devotion. These were sometimes introduced by
missionaries at the time of the initial evangelization, and
they often develop according to local custom.

The introduction of devotional practices into liturgical
celebrations under the pretext of inculturation cannot be
allowed "because by its nature, [the liturgy] is superior
to them."[97]

It belongs to the local Ordinary[98] to organize such devotions,
to encourage them as supports for the life and faith of
Christians, and to purify them when necessary, because

---

95   Cf. Vatican Council II, Constitution *Sacrosanctum Concilium*, n. 125; Dogmatic
     Constitution *Lumen gentium*, n. 67; *Code of Canon Law*, can. 1188.

96   Council of Nicea II: Denz.-Schonm. 601; cf. St. Basil, *On the Holy Spirit*, XVIII, 45;
     Sources Chretiennes, 17, 194.

97   Vatican Council II, Constitution *Sacrosanctum Concilium*, n. 13.

98   Cf. *Code of Canon Law*, can. 839 § 2.

they need to be constantly permeated by the Gospel.[99] He will take care to ensure that they do not replace liturgical celebrations or become mixed up with them.[100]

C. Necessary Prudence

46. "Innovations should only be made when the good of the Church genuinely and certainly requires them; care must be taken that any new forms adopted should in some way grow organically from forms already existing."[101] This norm was given in the Constitution *Sacrosanctum Concilium* in relation to the restoration of the liturgy, and it also applies, in due measure, to the inculturation of the Roman rite. In this field changes need to be gradual and adequate explanation given in order to avoid the danger of rejection or simply an artificial grafting onto previous forms.

47. The liturgy is the expression of faith and Christian life, and so it is necessary to ensure that liturgical inculturation is not marked, even in appearance, by religious syncretism. This would be the case if the places of worship, the liturgical objects and vestments, gestures and postures let it appear as if rites had the same significance in Christian celebrations as they did before evangelization. The syncretism will be still

---

99　John Paul II, Apostolic Letter *Vicesimus quintus annus*, 4 December 1988, n. 18: AAS 81 (1989), 914.

100　Cf. *ibid.*

101　Vatican Council II, Constitution *Sacrosanctum Concilium*, n. 23.

worse if biblical readings and chants (cf. above, no. 26) or the prayers were replaced by texts from other religions, even if these contain an undeniable religious and moral value.[102]

48. The Constitution *Sacrosanctum Concilium* envisaged the admission of rites or gestures according to local custom into rituals of Christian initiation, marriage and funerals.[103] This is a stage of inculturation, but there is also the danger that the truth of the Christian rite and the expression of the Christian faith could be easily diminished in the eyes of the faithful. Fidelity to traditional usages must be accompanied by purification and, if necessary, a break with the past. The same applies, for example, to the possibility of Christianizing pagan festivals or holy places, or to the priest using the signs of authority reserved to the Heads of civil society or for the veneration of ancestors. In every case it is necessary to avoid any ambiguity. Obviously the Christian liturgy cannot accept magic rites, superstition, spiritism, vengeance or rites with a sexual connotation.

49. In a number of countries there are several cultures which coexist and sometimes influence each other in such a way as

---

102 These texts can be used profitably in the homily because it is one of the tasks of the homily "to show the points of convergence between revealed divine wisdom and noble human thought, seeking the truth by various paths" (John Paul II, Apostolic Letter *Dominicae Cenae*, 24 February 1980, n. 10: AAS 72 (1980), 137.

103 Nn. 65, 77, 81. Cf. *Ordo initiationis christianae adultorum*, Praenotanda, nn. 30-31, 79-81, 88-89; *Ordo celebrandi Matrimonium*, editio typica altera, Praenotanda, nn. 41-44; *Ordo exsequiarum*, Praenotanda, nn. 21-22.

to lead gradually to the formation of a new culture, while at times they seek to affirm their proper identity, or even oppose each other, in order to stress their own existence. It can happen that customs may have little more than folkloric interest. The Episcopal Conference will examine each case individually with care: They should respect the riches of each culture and those who defend them, but they should not ignore or neglect a minority culture with which they are not familiar. They should weigh up the risk of a Christian community becoming inward looking, and also the use of inculturation for political ends. In those countries with a customary culture, account must also be taken of the extent to which modernization has affected the people.

50. Sometimes there are many languages in use in the one country, even though each one may be spoken only by a small group of persons or a single tribe. In such cases a balance must be found which respects the individual rights of these groups or tribes, but without carrying to extremes the localization of the liturgical celebrations. It is also sometimes possible that a country may be moving toward the use of a principal language.

51. To promote liturgical inculturation in a cultural area bigger that one country, the Episcopal Conferences concerned must work together and decide the measures which have to be taken so that "as far as possible, there are not notable ritual differences in regions bordering on another."[104]

---

104 Vatican Council II, Constitution *Sacrosanctum Concilium*, n. 23.

IV. Areas of Adaptation in the Roman Rite

52. The Constitution *Sacrosanctum Concilium* had in mind an inculturation of the Roman rite when it gave *Norms* for the adaptation of the liturgy to the mentality and needs of different peoples, when it provided for a degree of adaptation in the liturgical books (cf. below, nos. 53- 61), and also when it envisaged the possibility of more profound adaptations in some circumstances, especially in mission countries (cf. below, nos. 63-64).

A. Adaptations in the Liturgical Books

53. The first significant measure of inculturation is the translation of liturgical books into the language of the people.[105] The completion of translations and their revision, where necessary, should be effected according to the directives given by the Holy See on this subject.[106] Different literary genres are to be respected, and the content of the texts of the Latin typical edition is to be preserved; at the same time the translations must be understandable to participants (cf. above, no. 39), suitable for proclamation and singing, with appropriate responses and acclamations by the assembly.

---

105 Cf. *ibid.*, nn. 36 §§ 2, 3, and 4; 54; 63.

106 Cf. John Paul II, Apostolic Letter *Vicesimus quintus annus*, 4 December 1988, n. 20: AAS 81 (1989), 916.

All peoples, even the most primitive, have a religious language which is suitable for expressing prayer, but liturgical language has its own special characteristics: It is deeply impregnated by the Bible; certain words in current Latin use (*"memoria," "sacramentum"*) took on a new meaning in the Christian faith. Certain Christian expressions can be transmitted from one language to another, as has happened in the past, for example in the case of *"ecclesia," "evangelium," "baptisma," "eucharistia."*

Moreover, translators must be attentive to the relationship between the text and the liturgical action, aware of the needs of oral communication and sensitive to the literary qualities of the living language of the people. The qualities needed for liturgical translations are also required in the case of new compositions, when they are envisaged.

54. For the celebration of the eucharist, the Roman Missal, "while allowing . . . for legitimate differences and adaptations according to the prescriptions of the Second Vatican Council," must remain "a sign and instrument of unity"[107] of the Roman rite in different languages. The General Instruction on the Roman Missal foresees that "in accordance with the Constitution on the Liturgy, each Conference of bishops has the power to lay down norms for its own territory that are suited to the traditions and

107 Cf. Paul VI, Apostolic Constitution *Missale romanum*, 3 April 1969: AAS 61 (1969), 221.

character of peoples, regions and different communities."[108]
The same also applies to the gestures and postures of the
faithful,[109] the ways in which the altar and the Book of the
Gospels are venerated,[110] the texts of the opening chants,[111]
the song at the preparation of the gifts[112] and the communion
song,[113] the rite of peace,[114] conditions regulating communion
with the chalice,[115] the materials for the construction of the
altar and liturgical furniture,[116] the material and form of
sacred vessels,[117] liturgical vestments.[118] Episcopal Conferences
can also determine the manner of distributing communion.[119]

---

108 *Missale Romanum*, Institutio Generalis, n. 6; cf. also *Ordo Lectionum Missae*, editio typica
altera, Praenotanda, nn. 111-118.

109 *Missale Romanum*, Institutio Generalis, n. 22.

110 Cf. *ibid.*, n. 232.

111 Cf. *ibid.*, n. 26.

112 Cf. *ibid.*, n. 50.

113 Cf. *ibid.*, n. 56i.

114 Cf. *ibid.*, n. 56b.

115 Cf. *ibid.*, n. 242.

116 Cf. *ibid.*, nn. 263 and 288.

117 Cf. *ibid.*, n. 290.

118 Cf. *ibid.*, nn. 304, 305, 308.

119 *De Sacra Communione et de Cultu Mysterii Eucharistici Extra Missam*, Praenotanda, n. 21.

55. For the other sacraments and for sacramentals, the Latin typical edition of each ritual indicates the adaptations which pertain to the Episcopal Conferences,[120] or to individual bishops in particular circumstances.[121] These adaptations concern texts, gestures, and sometimes the ordering of the rite. When the typical edition gives alternative formulae, Conferences of Bishops can add other formulas of the same kind.

56. For the rites of Christian Initiation, Episcopal Conferences are "to examine with care and prudence what can properly be admitted from the traditions and character of each people"[122] and "in mission countries to judge whether initiation ceremonies practiced among the people, can be adapted into the rite of Christian Initiation, and to decide

---

120 Cf. *Ordo initiationis christianae adultorum*, Praenotanda generalia, nn. 30-33; Praenotanda, nn. 12, 20, 47, 64-65; Ordo, n. 312; Appendix, n. 12; *Ordo Baptismi parvulorum*, Praenotanda, nn. 8, 23-25; *Ordo Confirmationis*, Praenotanda, nn. 11-12, 16-17; *De sacra communione et de cultu mysterii eucharistici extra Missam*, Praenotanda, n. 12; *Ordo Paenitentiae*, Praenotanda, nn. 35b, 38; *Ordo Unctionis infirmorum eorumque pastoralis curae*, Praenotanda, nn. 38-39; *Ordo celebrandi Matrimonium*, editio typica altera, Praenotanda, nn. 39-44; *De Ordinatione Episcopi, presbyterorum et diaconorum*, editio typica altera, Praenotanda, n. 11; *De Benedictionibus*, Praenotanda Generalia, n. 39.

121 Cf. *Ordo initiationis christianae adultorum*, Praenotanda, n. 66; *Ordo Baptismi parvulorum*, Praenotanda, n. 26; *Ordo Paenitentiae*, Praenotanda, n. 39; *Ordo celebrandi Matrimonium*, editio typica altera, Praenotanda, n. 36.

122 *Ordo initiationis christianae adultorum*, *Ordo Baptismi parvulorum*, Praenotanda Generalis, n. 30, 2.

whether they should be used."[123] It is necessary to remember, however, that the term "initiation" does not have the same meaning or designate the same reality when it is used of social rites of "initiation" among certain peoples or when it is contrary to the process of Christian initiation, which leads through the rites of the catechumenate to incorporation into Christ in the church by means of the sacraments of baptism, confirmation and eucharist.

57. In many places it is the marriage rite that calls for the greatest degree of adaptation so as not to be foreign to social customs. To adapt it to the customs of different regions and peoples, each Episcopal Conference has the "faculty to prepare its own proper marriage rite, which must always conform to the law which requires that the ordained minister or the assisting layperson,[124] according to the case, must ask for and obtain the consent of the contracting parties and give them the nuptial blessing."[125] This proper rite must obviously bring out clearly the Christian meaning of marriage, emphasize the grace of the sacrament and underline the duties of the spouses.[126]

---

123 *Ibid.*, n. 31; cf. Vatican Council II, Constitution *Sacrosanctum Concilium*, n. 65.

124 Cf. *Code of Canon Law*, cann. 1108 and 1112.

125 Vatican Council II, Constitution *Sacrosanctum Concilium*, n. 77; *Ordo celebrandi Matrimonium*, editio typica altera, Praenotanda, n. 42.

126 Cf. Vatican Council II, Constitution *Sacrosanctum Concilium*, n. 77.

58. Among all peoples, funerals are always surrounded with special rites, often of great expressive value. To answer to the needs of different countries, the Roman ritual offers several forms of funerals.[127] Episcopal Conferences must choose those which correspond best to local customs.[128] They will wish to preserve all that is good in family traditions and local customs, and ensure that funeral rites manifest the Christian faith in the resurrection and bear witness to the true values of the Gospel.[129] It is in this perspective that funeral rituals can incorporate the customs of different cultures and respond as best they can to the needs and traditions of each region.[130]

59. The blessing of persons, places or things touches the everyday life of the faithful and answers their immediate needs. They offer many possibilities for adaptation, for maintaining local customs, and admitting popular usages.[131] Episcopal Conferences will be able to employ the foreseen dispositions and be attentive to the needs of the country.

---

127 Cf. *Ordo exsequiarum*, Praenotanda, n. 4.

128 Cf. *ibid.*, nn. 9 and 21, 1-3.

129 Cf. *ibid.*, n. 2.

130 Cf. Vatican Council II, Constitution *Sacrosanctum Concilium*, n. 81.

131 Cf. *ibid.*, 79; *De Benedictionibus*, Praenotanda Generalia, 39; *Ordo Professionis religiosae*, Praenotanda, nn. 12-15.

60. As regards the liturgical year, each particular Church and religious family adds its own celebrations to those of the universal Church, after approval by the Apostolic See.[132] Episcopal Conferences can also, with the prior approval of the Apostolic See, suppress the obligation of certain feasts or transfer them to a Sunday.[133] They also decide the time and manner of celebrating Rogationtide and Ember Days.[134]

61. The Liturgy of the Hours has as its goal the praise of God and the sanctification by prayer of the day and all human activity. Episcopal Conferences can make adaptations in the second reading of the Office of Readings, hymns and intercessions and in the final Marian antiphons.[135]

Procedure
62. When an Episcopal Conference prepares its own edition of liturgical books, it decides about the translations and also the adaptations which are envisaged by the law.[136] The acts of the Conference, together with the final vote, are signed by

---

132 Cf. *Normae universales de Anno liturgico et de calendario*, nn. 49, 55; S. Congregation for Divine Worship, Instruction *Calendaria particularia*, 24 June 1970: AAS 62 (1970), 349-370.

133 Cf. *Code of Canon Law*, can. 1246 § 2.

134 Cf. *Normae universales de Anno liturgico et de Calendario*, n. 46.

135 *Liturgia Horarum*, Institutio Generalis, nn. 92, 162, 178, 184.

136 Cf. *Code of Canon Law*, cann. 455 § 2 and 838 § 3; that is also the case for a new edition, cf. John Paul II, Apostolic Letter *Vicesimus quintus annus*, 4 December 1988, n. 20: AAS 81 (1989), 916.

the President and Secretary of the Conference and sent to the Congregation for Divine Worship and the Discipline of the Sacraments, along with two copies of the approved text.

Moreover along with the complete dossier should be sent:

a. A succinct and precise explanation of the reasons for the adaptations that have been introduced.

b. An indication as to which sections have been taken from other already approved liturgical books and which are newly composed.

After the recognition by the Apostolic See has been received, according to the law,[137] the Episcopal Conference promulgates the Decree and determines the date when the new text comes into force.

B. Adaptations Envisaged by No. 40 of the Conciliar Constitution on the Liturgy

63. Apart from the adaptations provided for in the liturgical books, it may be that "in some places and circumstances, an even more radical adaptation of the liturgy is needed, and this entails greater difficulties."[138] This is more than the sort of adaptations envisaged by the *General Instructions* and the *praenotanda* of the liturgical books.

---

137 *Code of Canon Law*, can. 838 § 3.

138 Vatican Council II, Constitution *Sacrosanctum Concilium*, n. 40.

It presupposes that an Episcopal Conference has exhausted all the possibilities of adaptation offered by the liturgical books; that it has made an evaluation of the adaptations already introduced and maybe revised them before proceeding to more far-reaching adaptations.

The desirability or need for an adaptation of this sort can emerge in one of the areas mentioned above (cf. nos. 53-61) without the others being affected. Moreover, adaptations of this kind do not envisage a transformation of the Roman rite, but are made within the context of the Roman rite.

64. In some places when there are still problems about the participation of the faithful, a bishop or several bishops can set out their difficulties to their colleagues in the Episcopal Conference and examine with them the desirability of introducing more profound adaptations, if the good of souls truly requires it.[139]

It is the function of Episcopal Conferences to propose to the Apostolic See the modifications it wishes to adopt following the procedure set out below.[140]

The Congregation for Divine Worship and the Discipline of the Sacraments is ready to receive the proposals of Episcopal

---

139 Cf. S. Congregation for Bishops, *Directory on the Pastoral Ministry of Bishops*, 22 February 1973, n. 84.

140 Cf. Vatican Council II, Constitution *Sacrosanctum Concilium*, n. 40, 1.

Conferences and examine them, keeping in mind the good of the local Churches concerned and the common good of the universal Church, and to assist the process of inculturation where it is desirable or necessary. It will do this in accordance with the principles laid down in this Instruction (cf. above, nos. 33-51), and in a spirit of confident collaboration and shared responsibility.

Procedure
65. The Episcopal Conference will examine what has to be modified in liturgical celebrations because of the traditions and mentality of peoples. It will ask the national or regional liturgical commission to study the matter and examine the different aspects of the elements of local culture and their eventual inclusion in the liturgical celebrations. The commission is to ensure that it receives the appropriate expert advice. It may be sometimes opportune to ask the advice of members of non-Christian religions about the religious or civil value of this or that element (cf. above, nos. 30-32).

If the situation requires it, this preliminary examination will be made in collaboration with the Episcopal Conferences of neighboring countries or those with the same culture (cf. above, nos. 33-51).

66. The Episcopal Conference will present the proposal to the Congregation, before any experimentation takes place. The presentation should include a description of the innovations proposed, the reasons for their adoption, the criteria used, the

times and places chosen for a preliminary experiment and an indication of which groups will make it, and finally the acts of the discussion and the vote of the Conference.

After an examination of the proposal carried out together by the Episcopal Conference and the Congregation, the latter will grant the Episcopal Conference a faculty to make an experiment for a definite period of time, where this is appropriate.[141]

67. The Episcopal Conference will supervise the process of experimentation,[142] normally with the help of the national or regional liturgical commission. The Conference will also take care to ensure that the experimentation does not exceed the limits of time and place that were fixed. It will also ensure pastors and the faithful know about the limited and provisional nature of the experiment, and it will not give it publicity of a sort which could have an effect on the liturgical practice of the country. At the end of the period of experimentation, the Episcopal Conference will decide whether it matches up to the goal that was proposed or whether it needs revision, and it will communicate its conclusions to the Congregation along with full information about the experiment.

---

141 Cf. *ibid.*, n. 40, 2.

142 Cf. *ibid.*

68. After examining the dossier, the Congregation will issue a decree giving its consent, possibly with some qualifications, so that the changes can be introduced into the territory covered by the Episcopal Conference.

69. The faithful, both lay people and clergy, should be well informed about the changes and prepared for their introduction into the liturgical celebrations. The changes are to be put into effect as circumstances require, with a transition period if this is appropriate (cf. above, no. 61).

Conclusion

70. The Congregation for Divine Worship and the Discipline of the Sacraments presents these rules to the Episcopal Conferences to govern the work of liturgical inculturation envisaged by the Second Vatican Council as a response to the pastoral needs of peoples of different cultures. Liturgical inculturation should be carefully integrated into a pastoral plan for the inculturation of the Gospel into the many different human situations that are to be found. The Congregation for Divine Worship and the Discipline of the Sacraments hopes that each particular Church, especially the young Churches, will discover that the diversity of certain elements of liturgical celebrations can be a source of enrichment, while respecting the substantial unity of the Roman rite, the unity of the whole Church and the integrity of the faith transmitted to the saints for all time (cf. Jude 3).

The present Instruction was prepared by the Congregation for Divine Worship and the Discipline of the Sacraments, by order of His Holiness Pope John Paul II, who approved it and ordered that it be published.

From the Congregation for Divine Worship and the Discipline of the Sacraments, 25 January 1994.

Cardinal Antonio M. Javierre Ortas
Prefect

† Archbishop Geraldo Agnelo
Secretary